CISTERCIAN STUDIES SERIES: NUMBER ONE HUNDRED SIXTY-ONE

A Gathering of Friends
The Learning and Spirituality of
John of Forde

Hilary Costello
Christopher Holdsworth

editors

CISTERCIAN STUDIES SERIES: NUMBER ONE HUNDRED SIXTY-ONE

A GATHERING OF FRIENDS

The Learning and Spirituality of
John of Forde

edited by

Hilary Costello
Christopher Holdsworth

Cistercian Publications
Kalamazoo, Michigan

Acknowledgements
The editors and publisher express their appreciation to the
Conway Library, Courtauld Institute of Art, London, and to
Dr Lindy Grant of the Conway Library, for providing the
photographs of Forde Abbey used in this volume.

The work of Cistercian Publications is made possible in part
by support from Western Michigan University to
The Institute of Cistercian Studies

Memoriae affectuosae monachi amabilis,
Edmundi Mikkers, qui nos conservos
ad Johannis de Forda opera, iugiter
spirantes Jesum, trahere laboravit,
hoc volumen piissime dedicamus.

Table of Contents

JOHN OF FORDE became a contender for an important place in medieval history when, in 1933, Dom Maurice Bell published his *Life of Wulfric of Haselbury, by John Abbot of Ford*. This made a major contribution to our knowledge of this particular hermit and of life in a small Somerset village in the early twelfth century, as well as of the eremitic movement in England. It has, however, remained largely unknown to all but a few scholars, partly because no complete translation has yet appeared, and also because of the difficulty of the latin text.

Bell published at a time when the the name of the monastery where John spent most of his life, and from which he takes his name, was spelled without a final 'e'. Similar usage is found in David Knowles' great *The Monastic Order in England*, but in two later works relating to english monasteries and their heads, he changed to the modern topographical spelling. That usage is followed here, even though both the editors, and others, have used the old spelling in previous publications. The appearance of Forde here is designed to erase any suggestion that John may have been related to any family called 'Ford' in Somerset, or elsewhere, and it is fervently hoped that no one may be tempted at a later date to advance the erroneous thesis that there were two Johns.

Apart from Bell's solitary work, little serious scholarship had been done on John until Christopher Holdsworth completed a Cambridge doctoral thesis in 1959 with the title 'Learning and Literature of English Cistercians, 1167–1214, with special reference to John of Ford'. This thesis, still unpublished, examined the literary tradition among the white monks in England, and, after moving on to a detailed account of John's life, provided an analysis of his approach to Scripture, and of his spiritual teaching as found in his sermons on the Song of Songs.

In 1970–71, the sermons themselves were edited by Edmund Mikkers and Hilary Costello, and subsequently translated into English by Sister Wendy Mary Becket. Since then a few articles have appeared on various aspects of John's teaching but no major study has been written.

The idea of a colloquium devoted solely to John should then be welcomed as a major breakthrough in the study of John. Proposed by Sister Elizabeth Oxenham and mounted by Christopher Holdsworth in 1991 to celebrate the eight-hundreth anniversary of the beginning of John's abbacy at Forde, this took place in the lovely setting of the Devon Centre at Dartington College, near Totnes in Devon from 28 June to 1 July 1991. A number of well-known medieval scholars from both sides of the Atlantic attended and contributed the papers which have now been gathered together in this present volume. One scholar who contributed an enormous amount to our knowledge of John, Father Edmond Mikkers, was unfortunately prevented by illness from being at Dartington. Since the colloquium, he has died, and this volume is dedicated to his memory.

Although John's two major works were at the heart of the meeting, interesting and lively papers which could not be included here explored other aspects of the historical context: David Bell, 'The Library at Forde'; Pietro De Leo, '*Regnum et Sacerdotium* in John of Forde'; David Park, 'A newly discovered *Crucifixion* at Forde and other recent advances in knowledge of Cistercian wall-painting and panel-painting in the British Isles'; and Andrew Pyle, 'The Estates of Forde.' Besides hearing and discussing papers, participants visited Exeter Cathedral, Haslebury, and Forde Abbey, where David Park and Laurence Kean guided the party.

This book begins with Christopher Holdsworth's introduction to the Colloquium, which raises a question that may not occur to the average reader: why did John of Forde became a writer at all? The question provides an opportunity to examine the literary and historical background to his works and to set them within the context of the cistercian movement in the twelfth century. Forde during his time was perhaps one of the most learned abbeys of the Order, in England rivalled only by Rievaulx, and boasted, amongst others in the community, John's immediate predecessor as abbot, Baldwin, later bishop of Worcester and archbishop of Canterbury. This opening paper, then, puts John into the framework of cistercian history and provides the reader with a background for his two major surviving writings.

'The Life of Wulfric of Haslebury' was the earlier of these two works and perhaps the one that has the most immediate appeal. Here Pauline Matarasso reveals a wonderfully sympathetic reading of this Life, in which she enters deeply into John's psychology and brings to life the people he describes in a vivid manner. We feel that we get to know these people in a personal way. They become our friends, or at least people we might meet in ordinary life. She demonstrates that the miracles and other stories are not just the normal fare of hagiographical literature, but are real events that have a real historical content. That is not to say that they should all be regarded as history in the way that we might think of it today. They inform us about the perceptions of men and women in the middle ages.

Another side of the 'Life' attracted Marsha Dutton; the way that it enabled John to express his own ideas about the nature of the contemplative life in his picture of the anchorite Wulfric. The history of the tensions in monasticism between the eremitic and coenobitic life and of the strains felt by Cistercians between the lives of action and contemplation form the background to this stimulating paper. Its centre is a careful analysis of each part of the 'Life' which ends with a comparison between passages from the 'Life' and others from the later sermons on the Song of Songs which shows the coherence of John's ideas, besides revealing Wulfric as both contemplative and man of action and service.

The next section of the book contains five papers which in various ways arise from study of John's later and major work, his 120 sermons on the Song of Songs.

One way of studying this work is to take a particular theme and bring together John's treatment of the subject. Father Hilary Costello takes the Fourth Gospel as such a theme. One can discern a certain predilection for this Gospel in John's writings. Three themes in particular were examined: the first, the Word of God in the bosom of the Father, is a focal point for the theology of the Father and the Son and their relationship within the Trinity. But John uses the phrase also to express the intimate way in which the Father and the Son look at the Church and the Blessed Virgin out of their own love. Secondly, in invoking the Word as the ultimate source of Love John of Forde concentrates particularly on Christ's love of the Church, a theme which holds an important place in these sermons. The third theme, 'The Word', invites a reflection on some of those great moments of joy in these sermons where John looks at God's glory in heaven, but at the same time tempers this joy with the realization that the Word, as Jesus the man, underwent the passion and death of the Cross.

Sister Elizabeth Oxenham concentrates on John's teaching about the jewish people. In spite of John's stringent condemnation of the jewish manner of interpreting the scriptures, he show himself acutely sympathetic to the Jews in stressing time and again their ultimate capacity to receive the deep spiritual message that God has reserved for them. In John's terms this is expressed by the theme 'The Return of the Jews at the end of time', which is probably all that he could say in his own day, given the atrocious background of anti-semitism that was rife in England and elsewhere throughout the twelfth century. All the more remarkable then is it that he envisages a divine and angelic enthusiasm as Christ sees the Jews leaping and somersaulting with joy before the Lord. Such a theme is perhaps unusual for a monastic writer at that time.

David Bell explores just what may have lain behind John's distrust of jewish biblical interpretation, and whether the virulence with which he expressed himself may not have been fueled by enthusiasm for it among his cistercian contemporaries. This suggestion, originally made by Christopher Holdsworth in his thesis, is well and truly laid to rest, but in its place something much more interesting emerges. Interest in jewish argument and exegesis was, as Bell puts it, 'the rule rather than the exception in the twelfth century' and often related to this was an interest in the literal meaning of the Bible, most evidently among the Victorines and Paris masters like Peter Comestor, Peter the Chanter and Stephen Langton. John had, therefore, in his sights a much wider target, and emerges as someone who was trying to turn back an irresistible force.

Bell's discussion ends with some comparison between John's commentary on the Song and that of his exact contemporary Alexander Nequam (Neckham). This theme is central to Christopher Holdsworth's contribution, which looks at the ways in which John of Forde and his much better-known augustinian contemporary expounded the Song. Nequam's considerable commentary, surviving in far more manuscripts than John's, but still unedited, emerges as belonging very much to the tradition which was based on a serious interest in the literal text, including the light thrown on it by jewish exegesis, although, like John, he also explored the various levels of spiritual meaning, including a reading of the whole Song as being concerned with the Virgin Mary as Bride. At the end, the interesting but unresolved question is raised whether John and Alexander may not have influenced each other, and whether Alexander's warm opinion of the Cistercians may not have arisen from his knowledge of John of Forde.

A quite new series of questions is raised by the short paper of Avril Henry: whether John's interpretation of the very last verse of the Song may not lie behind one section of the *The Mirour of Mans Saluacioune*. This anonymous fifteenth-century Middle English translation of the very well known and widely distributed *Speculum humanae salvationis* contains what so-far appears to be the sole evidence that anyone read John's commentary in the later middle ages, and that by that time it was circulating under the far better known name of Saint Bernard. Dr Henry, therefore, has opened up a number of avenues for further research.

Finally, Mother Beverly Aitken, gives a very personal expression of her gratitude to this master of the spiritual life. He is a guide of considerable charm because he speaks to us from 'the depths of his own experience', and this experience is all the more reliable for us to follow because he focuses on Christ's self-emptying in a way that should have a special appeal for us today. If we add to this John's affectionate tenderness for those who are spiritually weak or frail, we see at once how appealing his teaching is, how helpful for us to follow. 'I find him' she says, 'a lovably generous and compassionate person.'

By the end of the colloquium those who took part all felt that they knew far more about John than they had known before, and that even though their estimates of his work varied quite considerably, they were drawn towards him with a feeling of friendship: hence the title of this collection. But it also became clear to them that there are many sides of this interesting individual still to be revealed by further work. We need, for example, studies of his language and style, something mentioned once or twice in these papers, but not really discussed. We need, too, further studies of his exegetical method, of the degree of his dependence upon his predecessors, particularly among those of his own Order. A thorough comparison of his commentary and that of Saint Bernard would no doubt be useful, as would examination of the kind of biblical text which he used, and of the parts of the Bible to which he most frequently made appeal. Much of the breadth of his spiritual teaching remains unexplored, and again much might be learnt from a comparison of it with the writings of his near contemporaries, as, for example, the writer of the vernacular *Ancrene Wisse*. The uniqueness of the apparently single manuscript of his sermons should receive further study in the wake of Avril Henry's paper; could other copies of his sermons on the Song be found lurking under the name of his illustrious forerunner?

We hope that this book will be useful to many kinds of reader, to scholars as well as to religious, to ordinary persons interested in the past and to those hoping to find help in their own journeys. As we end this introduction we want to thank all the contributors to it for their patience and courtesy, not least to Finbarr Donovan who has prepared the indices, so making the book all the more easy to use.

Hilary Costello
Christopher Holdsworth

LIST OF ABBREVIATIONS

General Abbreviations

AASS	Acta Sanctorum
CF	Cistercian Fathers Series, Spencer, MA; Washington, D.C.; Kalamazoo, MI, 1970–
CCCM	Corpus Christianorum Continuatio Mediaevalis, Turnhout, 1966ff
ET	English Translation
PL	J. P. Migne, *Patrologiae cursus completus, series latina,* 221 vols. Paris, 1844–64
PLG	P. Glorieux, 'Pour revaloriser Migne,' *Mélanges* de *Science Réligieuse* 9 (1952)

The Works of Aelred of Rievaulx

Iesu	*De Iesus puero duodenni* (On Jesus at the Age of Twelve)
Inst incl	*De institutione inclusarum* (Rule for a Recluse)

The Works of Bernard of Clairvaux

SBOp	*Sancti Bernardi Opera,* edd. J. Leclercq, H. M. Rochais, C. H. Talbot, 8 vols. in 9. Rome 1957–77.
Circ	*Sermo in circumcisione Domini* (Sermon on the feast of the Circumcision)
Div	*Sermones de diversis* (Sermons on Various Subjects)
SC	*Sermones Super Cantica Canticorum* (Sermons on the Song of Songs)

15

The Works of John of Forde

Cant Serm   *Sermones CXX super extremam partem Cantici Canticorum* (Sermons on the Song of Songs)

Wulf   *The Life of Wulfric of Haselbury*

The Works of William of Saint Thierry

Ep frat   *Epistola [aurea] ad fratres de Monte Dei* (The Golden Epistle, The Letter to the Brethren on Mont Dieu)

_____

John of Forde 1191–1991

THE PURPOSE of this paper is to provide an introduction to the man whose life and work is the centre of this book, as it was of the colloquium at which all the papers here printed were first given. The subject suggested itself to some of those who attended the Cistercian Studies Conference at Kalamazoo in 1989, for two reasons: because the eight hundredth anniversary of the time when John became abbot of Forde would fall in 1991, and, as far as we were aware, no group of people had ever sat down together to share their ideas about him. And there seemed a need to do so, for in the previous thirty years or so, more attention had been given to John than had probably ever before been the case. It ultimately fell to me, as the organizer of the colloquium, to speak first, and hence to appear first in this book, partly because no one else volunteered to do so, and partly because I welcomed the opportunity to explore some general issues about John which I suspected might not be explored in any of the papers which followed. This suspicion was largely fulfilled and so this first chapter in the present book reproduces almost entirely what I then said, with a certain amount of editing to suit an audience of readers.

The general area which seems to me to need some comment is why John of Forde became a writer—after all very few abbots did attempt to leave any writings behind them, save, in many cases, legal and administrative records relating to the hold of their abbey upon its estates, and to the ways that these were exploited.[1] Scarcely an

---

1. A superficial view for one period emerges from seeing how few monks occur in J. C. Russell's *Dictionary of Writers of Thirteenth Century England*, Special Supplement 3, *Bulletin of the Institute of Historial Research* (London, 1936).

abbot did not set his hand to some charter conveying land, but only a handful have left original compositions. Few abbots composed *Lives* of holy persons, contemporary with themselves or earlier than their time, few left sermons behind them, fewer still extensive works of spiritual teaching. Why was this?

We may well start by admitting that few in any age, in any setting, even, dare one say it, in an institution of higher learning, actually write an original work of any length, still less one which survives into, and is read in, a later age. Beyond this we may remind ourselves that few monasteries, Cassiodorus's Vivarium apart, were designed as centres of scholarship and writing. None of the formative monastic Rules included writing among the activities in which they expected monks to engage, but we know that over the centuries not a few monks did compose works of many kinds: indeed in many senses most of the literature created in Western Europe between say 500 and 1100 which has survived was the achievement of monks.[2] But even so, monastic writers were a very small class in comparison with monastic readers.

In John's case there were some formal barriers against writing at all. The Order to which he belonged seems to have thought, from an early point in its history, that composition was an activity which should only take place with permission. In this it approached writing just as it did many other aspects of monastic life. We find among the so-called Statutes of 1134 one which reads 'No abbot or monk or novice is permitted to make a book (*libros facere*), unless it be allowed him in the General Chapter of abbots'.[3] In 1175 the General

2. See the recent discussion by Ludo J. R. Milis, *Angelic Monks and Earthly Men* (Woodbridge, 1992) 92–114.

3. *Statuta Capitulorum Generalium Ordinis Cisterciensis*, 1, ed. J. M. Canivez (Louvain, 1933) p. 26. Statute LVIII for the year 1134. [Hereafter abbreviated 1134/LVIII, with page number]. The dating of the early statutes is still provisional. Kovacs first drew attention to the fact that Manrique seems to have attributed one group to 1134 (F. Kovacs, 'A propos de la date de la rédaction des *Institute Generalis Capituli*', *Analecta Sacri Ordinis Cisterciensis* 7 (1951) 85–90. We may note that Baldwin, writing some time after 1178, inserted a reference to the prohibition into the preface of his *De commendatione fidei* in terms which suggest he thought it was not still

Chapter extended this provision to the writers of sermons, and other collections of writings.[4] The rationale behind such regulations, one may deduce, was that authorship sat rather awkwardly with monastic virtues like humility, or with keeping one's mind free of distractions when engaged in the basic monastic activity, prayer. Saint Bernard, we recall, told one of his correspondents that 'scribbling' was not something which fitted in with the silence of Lent.[5] So if (and it may be a big IF should Lekai be right in suggesting that even at this time no statute of the Chapter would take effect until it was reaffirmed at a subsequent chapter[6]) such legislation were followed in the whole cistercian family, no white monk would be likely to start to compose a book without some kind of authorization from above. There were, therefore, restraints upon any monk deciding to compose anything substantial, and peculiar restraints upon any cistercian. It is this whole background which raises the question: why did John become a writer?

But before we approach that major theme, it is worthwhile to pause for a moment upon a preliminary point: how do we know anything about our subject, how is it that there is anything to say about John? The question may seem such an obvious one as not to be worthy of attention, but I hope to convince you otherwise. This preliminary question also has the virtue that it provides a chance to recall our debt to earlier generations of scholars, and to some of our day who for reasons of age and distance could not be with us.

---

in force: 'Nam *tunc* temporis nos eiusdem Ordinis monachi, sine licentia scribere non sinebamur . . . .' [my emphasis], *Balduini de Forda Sermones De Commendatione Fidei*, ed. David N. Bell, CCCM 909 (Turnholt: Brepols, 1991) 345, and (for date) xxx.

4. *Statuta* 1175/31; Canivez 1:84.

5. Ep. 89.1 (to Oger); SBOp 7:235 (ET *The Letters of St. Bernard of Clairvaux*, letter 92, trans. Bruno Scott James [London-Notre Dame, 1953] 137–138. His interesting reflections on how disturbing composition was were themselves written in Lent.

6. Louis J. Lekai, O.Cist., 'Ideals and Reality in Early Christian Life and Legislation', *Cistercian Ideals and Reality*, Cistercian Studies Series 60, ed. John R. Sommerfeldt (Kalamazoo, 1978) 4–29, esp. 18.

There was material for the colloquium, and for this book, because some of John of Forde's own writings have survived. Without his *Life of Wulfric*, or the Sermon-commentary on the Song of Songs there would be little to say. If we were to print out on paper all the evidence for his existence apart from that produced by his own pen, the facts would not cover many sheets. References to the abbot of Forde from his time in either royal or episcopal or cistercian records are few, though fairly extensive in comparison with those for many other abbots of his day.[7] Something could, and indeed will, be said later about the setting in which he lived and worked, the buildings of his home, Forde abbey, the library which those buildings contained, and about the estates from which the community he guided drew its income, but without his own writings there would be little to flesh out those architectural, bibliographical and economic studies. So it is worth realizing, how very slender is the corpus of manuscripts upon which our knowledge of him rests. Four manuscripts survive for his *Life of Wulfric*, but only one for his greatest work, the *Commentary on the Song of Songs*, and one for his short, isolated sermon for Palm Sunday.[8] It would be a splendid result of this book if it led someone to discover more manuscripts, in which John may now be hidden under the veil of anonymity or the name of some better-known writer.

The relatively rich manuscript tradition of the *Life of Wulfric* reflects the popularity of hagiographical works and springs from the extraordinary place which hermits, anchorites, and recluses played in England in the twelfth century.[9] Interest in isolated holy

7. There is a summary in the introduction to the latin edition of the commentary by Edmund Mikkers and Hilary Costello, *Iohannis de Forda: Super extremam partem Cantici canticorum sermones cxx*, volume 1, CCCM 17: viii–xi, and a more extensive one in Costello's Introduction to volume one of Wendy Mary Beckett's translation, *John of Ford: Sermons on the Song of Songs*, 1, Cistercian Fathers Series 29 (Kalamazoo, 1977) 3–10.

8. *Wulfric of Haselbury by John, abbot of Ford*, Somerset Record Society 47, ed. Dom Maurice Bell (1933) lxxvii-lxxxii; Mikkers and Costello, Introduction to Cant Serm, xiii, xx–xxiii.

9. See the articles by Pauline Matarasso and Marsha Dutton below, and also Ann K. Warren, *Anchorites and their Patrons in Medieval England*

men and women was perhaps as strong then as it had been in the Mediterranean world of the fourth and fifth centuries. But the interest in records of such people remained at so high a level throughout the Middle Ages that even if the original manuscripts of John's Life of Wulfric had disappeared, we should still know at least a potted version of what he wrote through the *Sanctilogium* of John of Tynemouth, compiled early in the fourteenth century. That was used in its turn by John Capgrave (d. 1454) a century later, and Capgrave's version was used by Wynkyn de Worde in his *Nova Legenda Anglie*, printed in 1516.[10] But John's other works, so far as we yet know, survive in single manuscripts, and his most extensive work seems to have cast scarcely a shadow on later writers. I use the phrase 'scarcely a shadow' since Dr Henry introduces us to what may be no more than a faint print of that shadow which has never been seen before.[11]

For the survival of the commentary on the Song, we surely must celebrate the name of William Gray, bishop of Ely from 1454 to 1478, for it was he who gave the single manuscript to Balliol College. Without him where would we be? He is known as a collector of classical and medieval manuscripts,[12] and for John's work his interest was crucial, although a half century after Gray's time, during the dissolution of the monasteries, that great book-lover and antiquary, John Leland, saw at least two other manuscripts of John's commentary, at Forde and Beaulieu.[13] There is no difficulty in explaining

---

(Berkeley, Los Angeles, London: University of California Press, 1985), and Christopher Holdsworth, 'Hermits and the Powers of the Frontier' in *Saints and Saints' Lives: Essays in Honour of D. H. Farmer*, Reading Medieval Studies 16 (Reading, 1990) 55–76.

10. Bell discusses the later literary history, pp. lxiv-lxxiii. He does not mention Nicholas Roscarrock (*c.* 1548–1634), another who mentions Wulfric: *Nicholas Roscarrock's Lives of the Saints of Cornwall and Devon*, Devon and Cornwall Record Society, New Series 35, ed. Nicholas Orme (1992) 196.

11. See pp. 175–188 below.

12. R. A. B. Mynors, *Catalogue of the Manuscripts of Balliol College* (Oxford, 1963) xxiv–xlv.

13. J. Leland, *Antiquarii de rebus britannicis collectanea*, ed. T. Hearne (London, 1770) 4:150, 149.

why Forde had a copy, but Beaulieu perhaps needs a pause. Could they have been interested in the work because of its reference to that complex figure, king John, who besides being a hammer of the Cistercians during the Interdict, was also their own royal founder?[14]

Be that as it may, interest in John of Forde and any of his works was scant between William Gray's or Leland's day and our own. Compilers of handbooks on medieval authors like bilious Bale, or his Catholic successor Pits,[15] usually confused John with other writers, and not one of his works was available in full until Dom Maurice Bell, a monk of Downside, brought out the *Life of Wulfric* in 1933. His impulse seems to have been partly local *pietas*, concern for a holy person who had long before lived in Somerset, the county in which he himself lived. Forde itself, in the parish of Thorncombe, was not in John's time (or now) in Somerset, but lay in an isolated pocket of Devonshire surrounded by Dorset until a tidying up of boundaries in the nineteenth century,[16] but Haselbury has always been in Somerset. Downside in Bell's day contained within its walls a number of serious scholars, concerned to rediscover the history of monasticism in England; of them the most significant was to be David Knowles.[17] In 1933 he was in the early stages of the work which was to lead to the appearance of perhaps his most successful

14. Cf. C. J. Holdsworth, 'John of Ford and the Interdict', *English Historical Review* 78 (1963) 705–714; *idem.* 'Royal Cistercians: Beaulieu, her Daughters and Rewley', in *Thirteenth Century England IV: Proceedings of the Newcastle upon Tyne Conference 1991*, edd. P. A. Coss and S. Lloyd (Woodbridge, 1992) 139–150.

15. John Bale 1489–1563 earned his name from his vituperative comments on his former co-religionists in his *Scriptorum illustrium majoris Brytanniae* (Basle, 1557), whilst John Pits, or Pitseus, 1560–1616 spent most of his life in exile and based his *Relationum Historicarum de Rebus Anglicis* (Paris, 1619) on Bale, whom he detested. See *Dictionary of National Biography*, ed. Leslie Stephen and Sidney Lee (Oxford, Oxford University Press, 1917 ff) I, 961–962 and XV, 1225–1226.

16. The changes in the boundaries of Devon are summarised in W.G. Hoskins, *Devon* (Newton Abbot, new edition, 1972) 10–11.

17. Adrian Morey, *David Knowles: A Memoir* (London, 1979) 117–124; Christopher Brooke in Christopher Brooke, Roger Lovatt, David Luscombe, and Aelred Sillem, *David Knowles Remembered* (Cambridge, 1991) 4–19, 47–56.

Fig. 1 Exterior of east range from south west, with dormitory above and undercroft below.

Fig. 2   Detail of North Walk of Cloister showing original early thirteenth-century arcade behind.

single volume, *The Monastic Order in England*, published first in 1940. There the Life of Wulfric merits no more than a footnote, inserted into his rather longer account of Baldwin, to whom I shall return in a moment. Knowles spent no space at all on the commentary.[18]

Those Sermons were very little studied until the latin edition appeared nearly forty years after the Life was printed. But interest in it was piqued only five years after the *Vita* appeared, as early as 1938, when Edmond Mikkers edited the Prologue and first sermon in the then youthful periodical *Collectanea Ordinis Cisterciensium Reformatorum*.[19] A few years after Mikker's first anonymous *essai* at editing John appeared, the english scholar, Hugh Talbot, then still a Cistercian at Mount Saint Bernard, made the single Palm Sunday Sermon available in the same periodical, just as the war was ending in 1945.[20] Here the story begins to involve some of those who were at the colloquium, since it was Hilary Costello, also at Mount Saint Bernard, who undertook with Mikkers the mammoth task of editing the Commentary, which came out in the Corpus Christianorum in 1970.[21]

I came into the story myself somewhat earlier, if you will forgive a personal reminiscence, since I began to work on John in 1954, when Hugh Talbot suggested to my supervisor, David Knowles (then no longer at Downside, but a professor at Cambridge), that the commentary would be a good subject for a thesis. Throughout the next five years until the thesis was completed, he remained a patient and helpful advisor, and I feel a large debt for his original suggestion and continuing interest. In fact the thesis took shape under the guidance of Richard Hunt, then Keeper of Western Manuscripts

18. David Knowles, *The Monastic Order in England* (rpt. Cambridge, 1950) 317 n. 6; the second edition (1963) has my 1961 article in the Additional Bibliography.

19. 'Prologue and First Sermon to John of Ford's Commentary on the Song of Songs', *Collectanea Ordinis Cisterciensium Reformatorum* 5 (1938) 250–261. The article, by Mikkers, appears anonymously.

20. C. H. Talbot (also 'anonymous' here), 'Un sermon inédit de Jean de Ford', COCR 7 (1940–45) 36–45.

21. See the Table of Abbreviations for full details.

in the Bodleian, to whom Dom David handed me over when I went to Oxford in 1955 to work on the Balliol manuscript. The choice could not have been better for me, since from his study, then at one end of Duke Humfrey's Library, Richard could easily keep an eye on what I was trying to do as he walked past. And he had, of course, unrivalled experience with manuscripts and deep knowledge of the period.

My work between 1954 and 1960 resulted, as far as the wider world knew, in two articles: one a fairly general study on cistercian writing in John's day, and another editing the then unknown sermon on the Interdict.[22] By the time they appeared my interests were moving in other directions, largely, I suppose, because I began to feel that the material was difficult for someone with little theological training to deal with adequately, so I turned to the more earthy job of editing the early charters of another cistercian abbey, Rufford, in Nottinghamshire. I was, I think, too, somewhat depressed by the comment which one of the examiners of my thesis, Richard Southern, made *en passant* at my *viva* (a remark which may shock some, even though I think now that it reflects more on the dullness of my thesis rather than on John): 'It's a pity that John of Forde turned out to be such a bore'. At least that's what I think he said, although the strain of the occasion may well have distorted my memory. Certainly he made me feel that a book on John would not be of wide interest then, so my thesis stayed on the shelf, and did not appear in print. Since coming down to Exeter in 1977, my interest in John has taken a new lease of life, resulting in some new work, and, who knows, perhaps, in time, a new book, when Saint Bernard with whom I labour at present, will allow me.

But as my johannine interests waned, others', fortunately, were waxing. Mikkers and Costello started their edition, whose appearance was to be followed very shortly, between 1982 and 1987, by

22. C. J. Holdsworth, 'John of Ford and English Cistercian Writing 1167–1214', *Transactions of the Royal Historical Society*, 5th Series, 11 (1961) 117–136; and first article in note 14 above. The thesis was *Learning and Literature of English Cistercians 1167–1214, with special reference to John of Ford*, Cambridge University, Ph.D., 1959.

a complete translation by Wendy Beckett, occupying no less than seven volumes in the Cistercian Fathers Series.[23] The blessing that this has been will be readily appreciated by all of us here, since although John wrote, perhaps, less floridly in his latter days than he did in the *Life*, his Latin remains fairly complex for a modern reader. None of the papers that follow here tackle his style head on, although there are references to his length, and to his use of the Bible. Perhaps someone will be sufficiently interested by these present studies to explore his language, syntax and style further.

Having spoken of the recent tradition of scholarship on John and the thin thread of manuscripts upon which much of it has rested, let me return to my main question: why was John a writer? This now needs breaking down into a number of questions, which demand attention in turn. The first of these, surely, is why did he become a monk, and in particular why did he join the community at Forde? Then, we can move on to try to discover why he became a writer, and why he wrote on the themes which he chose.

I do not think that John anywhere explicitly mentions why he became a monk, nor why he entered Forde, but material to suggest the answer to both questions exists. But let us first try to fix his entry into the religious life in time. The evidence is complex, and the only certain information we have is that he was prior at Forde before the end of 1184, since he addressed his first preface for the *Life of Wulfric* to Bartholomew, bishop of Exeter, who died that year.[24] In his second preface, addressed to Baldwin, by then archbishop of Canterbury, he says that Bartholomew had approved his intention of writing on Wulfric, 'asked by the lord abbot of blessed memory . . . .'[25] The words are not entirely without ambiguity, but Bell, I think rightly, took them to refer to an intervention with the bishop made by an abbot dead by the time of writing, that is to say by around 1185. The most likely candidate is Robert of

23. For full details, see the Table of Abbreviations.
24. Wulf, p. 7.
25. Wulf, pp. 10–12: 'Consultus ergo a domino abbate, scilicet piae memoriae, Exoniae episcopus voluntatem non solum probavit sed et accendit . . .' p. 11.

Penington, second abbot of Forde and one of the original party from Waverley in Surrey who founded the community in 1136. He was elected before 1141, and was still in office when Baldwin joined the community, some time after September 1169, being replaced fairly soon by Baldwin himself, by 1175 at the latest.[26] John, therefore, seems to have gone to Forde during Robert's day, perhaps about the same time as Baldwin, conceivably a little earlier.

We may remind ourselves here that this was a time when monastic life was exercising the greatest attractive power which, perhaps, it ever has had, on both men and women in England, as in other parts of western Europe. Desire to embrace a disciplined form of retreat from secular society was motive helping to bring into existence a growing number of monasteries, the other being the concerns of patrons and benefactors for their own salvation, as well as for a number of less intangible things, like hospitality and influence over land and people.[27]

The kind of appeal which the monastery had for John and thousands of others can be sensed in a letter written by one of the monks in the community which he joined, a certain Roger. Roger had, at an earlier period in his life, been a pupil of Baldwin, and seems to have become a cistercian about the same time as his master.[28] The letter, addressed to a friend Galienus, is typical of its genre; it appeals to

26. David Knowles, C. N. L. Brooke, and Vera C. M. London, *The Heads of Religious Houses: England and Wales, 940–1216* (Cambridge, 1972) 132.

27. For that enthusiasm, see C. H. Lawrence, *Medieval Monasticism* (2nd edition London-New York: Longman, 1989) 149–205.

28. The relationship emerges from a Tournai MS destroyed in the Second World War, but fortunately catalogued: P. Faider and P. Van Sint Jan, *Catalogue des Manuscrits Conservés à Tournai, Catalogue Général des MSS des Bibliothèques de Belgique*, volume VI (Gembloux, 1950) 151. C. H. Talbot first edited the text, believing it then to be by Roger of Byland ('A Letter of Roger, Abbot of Byland', *Analecta Sacri Ordinis Cisterciensis* 7 [1951] 218–231). He drew my attention to the Tournai evidence, to which I referred in 'John of Ford' (1961, note 22 above) 125–126. Unfortunately the correction was missed by the late Lawrence C. Braceland, the translator of Gilbert of Hoyland, and so a translation of the letter to Galienus is now to be found ascribed to Roger in *Treatises, Epistles, and Sermons with a Letter of Roger of Byland 'The Milk of Babes'*, The Works of Gilbert of Hoyland 4, Cistercian Fathers Series 34 (Kalamazoo, 1981) 109–125.

Galienus to leave the world with its vain delights and pomps for the hard discipline of the cloister. It is packed with passages which pour scorn on those fleeting pleasures which must inevitably pass away and from which death may snatch the idler at any moment. Carnal love, the 'charm of wantonness and the banquets of merrymakers', 'the subtlety of logic or of some other vain knowledge' are denigrated by comparison with heavenly love, which will be safeguarded by the practices of 'our order', harsh as it may be, with its 'many . . . labours, its abstinences, endurance of cold, its fasts and vigils', as well as its abstemious food and drink, and still harsher clothing.[29] Whether John, like Galienus, could claim that he had been 'reared in the purple' and so needed special encouragement to adopt a scratchy habit, seems doubtful, but he must, presumably have been won over by arguments similar to those which Roger used with Galienus.

Just why John responded to this kind of appeal when he did, around 1169, we can not know for certain, as is true of so many other aspects of his life. But if he was a Devonian, possibly a fairly young man, studying in the schools attached to the cathedral in Exeter, it is at least highly likely that the crisis between archbishop Thomas Becket and the king had something to do with it.[30] The pressures felt by his own bishop, Bartholomew, were so great that he himself retired to a monastery for a year. The identity of the place he chose is not known, but in view of the fact that Baldwin, one of his archdeacons and no less than two of Baldwin's pupils went to Forde, it is surely not unlikely that their bishop went there too. In any case it is I think easy to connect John's retirement from the world with the same time of great tension. The struggle between *regnum* and *sacerdotium* made him feel that the choice of heavenly love was to be preferred to the pleasures of the world.

Just why Forde, rather than some other religious house in the diocese, attracted John he does not tell us, but again we can make some plausible suggestions. The fact that he did join the white monks indicates that there was something about the life of that order

29. *The Milk of Babes* 14.17; ET pp. 117, 119.
30. Cf. Christopher Holdsworth, 'Baldwin of Forde, Cistercian and Archbishop of Canterbury', *Friends of Lambeth Palace Library, Annual Report 1989*, pp. 16–17.

which peculiarly attracted him. Surviving evidence about monastic recruitment makes it likely that John would have been likely to look only fairly close at hand.[31] That being the case, there were in the 1160s only two cistercian monastieries within the diocese, both founded in 1136: Buckfast and Forde.[32] The former, on the site of an older benedictine foundation, was reformed that year by King Stephen to follow the customs of the norman monastery of Savigny, with which he was familiar from the mother house within his own county of Mortain. Stephen, indeed, had established what became the first and wealthiest english daughter of Savigny at Furness in Lancashire some time earlier, in 1124. By the time John was looking around for a home, Buckfast had been absorbed into the more successful reformed monasticism based on the way of life at Cîteaux, along with the rest of the Savigniac family in 1147. There is some evidence that the english houses in that family were not altogether content with this development, and it is possible that Buckfast was not, for this reason, a place which would attract a mature entrant. Almost nothing is known about the monastery in this period, so this must remain a mere suggestion. About Forde, on the other hand, much more, relatively, is known.

We have seen that Forde was attracting a number of people who left some writings behind them: Baldwin and Roger have already been mentioned. We can deduce that it was drawing good numbers of less conspicuous choir monks, and we may assume lay brothers also, because it was able to provide a colony to establish its first daughter house at Bindon in 1172. Since by that time the Order had

31. This statement is based on impressions from a number of cartularies, where, normally, very few monks actually appear. In my own *Rufford Charters*, 4 vols (Thoroton Society Record series, 29–30, 32, 34, 1972–1981) the names of 19 monks occur. Seven have a place-name as part of their name, of these five probably are from places in Nottinghamshire (where Rufford was) or in adjacent Lincolnshire: only two from more distant places. The subject needs further study.

32. The early history of the two houses is discussed in Christopher J. Holdsworth, 'The Cistercians in Devon', *Studies in Medieval History presented to R. Allen Brown*, edd. Christopher Harper-Bill, Christopher Holdsworth, and Janet L. Nelson (Woodbridge, 1989) 179–184.

Fig. 3   Interior view of undercroft to dorter looking north.

Fig. 4 East range, from north east, showing exterior of chapter house with late window inserted.

Fig 5 Original vault of chapter house.

laid down that no colonies were to be sent out unless a house had sixty monks within it, it is likely that Forde by 1172 held at least that number of religious, with, perhaps two to three times as many lay brothers.[33] In short it was a thriving community.

We know, on the other hand, that its beginnnings had been less bright. Within five years of its foundation at Brightley, on the edge of Dartmoor, the community had had to move to a gentler site in the parish of Thorncombe, in the valley of the Axe. There it found itself in very different country, not much like that which the Cistercians said they liked to settle in, since the new place was near to many old-established villages, scarcely suitable for the kind of exploitation based on granges, relatively withdrawn from the disciplines of communal agriculture, which the Order's early regulations said it wished to practise.[34] What may be significant for John's development is that from its start Forde seems to have had an unusually close relationship with its patrons.[35]

The founder was Richard FitzBaldwin, probably the wealthiest landholder in the region in the 1130s, and sheriff of the county of Devon. Brightley seems to have been the foundation of his old age, at a point when he had no sons of his own to inherit, a situation not uncommon in the period, and one which may well have created an interest for such a man in having monks pray for his soul, and thereby give his name some perpetual memory. About a third of cistercian houses founded in England before 1153 owed their existence to men without heirs, some of them childless by misfortune like Richard, some of them childless by profession since they were

33. *Statuta* 1134/unnumbered; Canivez 1:22 fn. This statute was included by Angelo Manriques in his '1134' collection, and numbered xxvii there (*Annales Cistercienses* [Lyon, 1642, rpt. Farnborough, 1970]) I:277. It has not often been noticed and needs more study to be placed chronologically. The proportion of choir monks to lay brothers can only be approximate; see *Walter Daniel's Life of Aelred of Rievaulx*, ed, and trans. F. M. Powicke (London, 1950 - Kalamazoo, 1994) p. 38 and note.

34. This is a very controversial question. For a recent discussion, see Constance Brittain Bouchard, *Holy Entrepreneurs: Cistercians, Knights, and Economic Exchange in Twelfth-Century Burgundy* (Ithaca-London: Cornell University Press, 1991).

35. See Holdsworth, 'Cistercians in Devon' (note 32 above) 182–184.

bishops.[36] Richard's sister and heiress, Adelicia (who even seems to have inherited his position as sheriff, calling herself *vicecomitissa*) saved the community at Brightley from disaster by offering them the new site near Thorncombe, taking back into her own hands in exchange their first home by the moor. But their first founder, so to say, followed them down, since his bones were removed to the new abbey. Within a few years patronage passed to the Courtenay family which kept a close interest in their abbey, normally ending their days by being buried alongside the high altar.[37] This relationship between patrons and their foundation may have helped to involve John as abbot with the outside world to a significant degree, something which, I will suggest, may have had a bearing upon his development as a writer.

Certainly Forde when John entered it must have been a stimulating place. Robert of Penington, by then old, in at least his sixties, must have had vivid memories of the difficult early times his community had experienced , as well as of their relationship to the local holy man, Wulfric. But the presence of Baldwin and the small group of writers around him, Roger already mentioned, and Maurinus his contemporary, must have made the possibility of John becoming a writer himself much more likely.

Baldwin was very productive during his years as monk and abbot, completing then the majority of his total output, in particular his treatise *De sacramento altaris*, as well as most of his shorter treatises. The evidence is not conclusive in the case of the *Treatises*, recently translated—and much more than that—by David Bell, but the fact that many of them seem to be aimed at a monastic audience makes it at least very likely that they were written at Forde, rather than, say, at Canterbury, a community with which he had such strained relations that he rarely stayed there.[38] During John's early years as a

36. *Ibid.* p. 191.
37. See the *Historia fundationis* of Forde, in William Dugdale, *Monasticon Anglicanum*, edd. Caley, Ellis, and Bandinel (London, 1816–1830) 5:377–378.
38. *Baldwin of Ford: Spiritual Tractates*, Cistercian Fathers Series 38, 41, trans. David N. Bell (Kalamazoo, 1986) 1:20. 'The great majority of

monk, Roger too was putting together his most important work, an account of the visions seen by a german nun, Elizabeth of Schönau, a work which was to play an important role in popularising belief in the bodily assumption of the Virgin Mary, since Elizabeth had 'seen' this in one of her visions.[39] Beside these two was the still shadowy monk Maurinus, who composed a short verse life of Thomas Becket, probably not long after Thomas's death, and who, like Roger, seems originally to have been a pupil of Baldwin. Besides these three, there was also a monk with an interest in collecting stories about the Virgin Mary: William who became abbot of Forde's first daughter house, Bindon, around 1180. One of the stories which he included in his huge, and still unexplored collection, was told him by John when abbot. Such people must have brought to Forde a real interest in books, and so helped to create there a significant library.[40] Here we may note that Alexander, who went from Forde to become abbot at Meaux in 1197, was remembered at his new community as a lover of books. Altogether, then, the setting where John spent most of his monastic career was one in which an interest in writing and in books was a natural thing, and, as we have already seen, this was a rather unusual thing for any monastic community, particularly, perhaps, for a cistercian house. One antiquary commented that Forde in John's time contained 'more learning than three convents of the same

---

the treatises–all but three–clearly derive from a monastic milieu'. For Bell's new latin edition, see note 3 above. I have reviewed one side of Baldwin's relations with Christ Church Canterbury in 'Baldwin of Forde' (note 30 above) 22–27.

39. Ruth J. Dean, 'Elizabeth of Schönau and Roger of Ford', *Modern Philology* 41 (1944) 209–220. There is a magnificent illustration of the bodily assumption in the York Psalter which may well derive from knowledge of Roger's edition. See T. S. R. Boase, *The York Psalter* (London, 1962) plate 6, opposite p. 26 and pp. 10–11.

40. See Holdsworth, 'John of Ford' (1961, note 22 above) 126, for Maurinus, other writers, and books at Ford. See too David N. Bell, *An Index of Authors and Works in Cistercian Libraries in Great Britain* (CS 130, Kalamazoo, 1992) 240 and *idem, The Libraries of the Cistercians, Gilbertines and Premonstratensians*, Corpus of British Medieval Library Catalogues 3 (British Library in association with British Academy, London, 1992) 27–28.

bigness anywhere in England'.[41] Whether he exaggerated or not, we can safely conclude that no other cistercian house in England was so productive between the last quarter of the twelfth century and first years of the thirteenth. Well might one call Forde the Rievaulx of the south during those years.[42]

Forde when John joined it was, then, a community with an active learned tradition, and this very fact may have been the crucial element in deciding him to go there rather than anywhere else. Without any doubt, once there he would have fond it relatively natural to develop what talents he might have had as a writer. His first commission, the *Life of Wulfric*, seems to have been undertaken, as we have noticed, with the encouragement not only of the abbot who led the community during his first years as a monk, but also with the general approval of the diocesan, Bartholomew.[43] Perhaps such authorisation fulfilled sufficiently the Order's regulations. But it was also a community which for most of the 1170s was dominated by one person, Baldwin, who besides being an author was also a canon lawyer of note.[44] He had been trained in this burgeoning discipline in Italy and had gone on to serve the see of Exeter as canon of the cathedral and utimately as archdeacon of Totnes (the town on whose edge we meet). It is not surprising, therefore, that his talent as a lawyer was not allowed to hide under a bushel once he became a monk. As early as 1185 he was appointed judge-delegate in a famous case concerning the exemption of the abbey of Malmesbury from episcopal oversight. During the following five years, until his election to the see of Worcester, Baldwin was used often as a papal judge, so much so that he seems to have begun to collect together papal decretals to help him in this work. This collection, now called the *Collectio Wigorniensis*, continued to be added to at later stages

41. Thomas Fuller, *History of the Worthies of England*, 3 vols. (London, 1840, ed. by P. Austin Nuttall) 1:421.

42. Apart from Walter Daniel, Rievaulx's only other monk-writer in John's day was Matthew the precentor; see André Wilmart, 'Les Mélanges de Mathieu préchantre de Rievaulx vers le debut du XIIIe siècle', *Revue Bénédictine* 52 (1940) 15–84.

43. See notes 24–25 above.

44. Cf. 'Baldwin of Forde' (note 30 above) 15–16, 19–20.

of his career. John, we may remember here, also served as a papal judge-delegate, not anything like as often as Baldwin, I think, but to a significant degree, and was also widely used by the General Chapter on disciplinary matters in 1200, 1205, 1206 and 1210 and 1213.[45] His skills as a mediator seem to have been valued particularly. In any case, he must often have been away from Forde on the Order's business. Between 1204 and 1207 his work as confessor and alms-giver to the king, which he owed to Hubert Walter, then archbishop of Canterbury, also took him away from his monks. By those years, too, Forde had a second daughter house, Dunkeswell, founded by that great royal servant (and Devonian) William Brewer.[46] The place was not far away from Forde, but its existence added a further weight, drawing John away from Forde from time to time.

What we are, I hope, beginning to see is that John was a man of many talents besides those of a writer, talents which were appreciated even by the distant pope, and by the Order to which he belonged. In this light, two things can be seen rather better: firstly, how it came about that he took up the formidable task of completing the commentary which Bernard had begun on the Song of Songs; and why that work is full of expression of regret for the tensions he felt between what he wanted to do and what he actually did. Let me now turn to these two matters and, perhaps, into an answer about his quality as writer.

The attempts made following Bernard's death in 1153 to find someone able and willing to bring his unfinished *magnum opus* to an end make a complex story.[47] The first man recruited, Gilbert of Hoyland, died in 1172 before he could complete the job, whilst

---

45. See Cant Serm ix–x, and my 'John of Ford' (note 22) 118–119 for this activity.

46. Holdsworth, 'Cistercians in Devon' (note 32 above) 184–185.

47. It is summarised by Mikkers and Costello, Cant Serm, pp. vii–viii. The story of Geoffreys' commentaries was first unravelled by Jean Leclercq 'Les écrits de Geoffrey d'Auxerre' in *Revue Bénédictine* 62 (1952) 274–291, and reprinted in his *Recueil d'études sur saint Bernard et ses écrits* 1 (Storia e Letteratura, Rome, 1962) 30–44, esp. 44. Since then Ferruccio Gastaldelli has edited them in the series *Temi e Testi* (Rome, 1974), which I have not seen.

Geoffrey of Auxerre, who was then asked by the abbot of Cîteaux to do so, insisted on starting again at the beginning, using some of his own earlier work as well as Bernard's and Gilbert's. Perhaps the result was never well-regarded in the Order, but it surely is significant that John began, not like Geoffrey at the beginning, but almost exactly where Gilbert had left off. Actually, he started with Chapter 5, verse eight, *Adiuro vos, filiae Jerusalem*, which was two verses into Gilbert's commentary, but John takes off into his spacious manner only with the next verse *Dilectus meus candidus et rubicundus*, for which Gilbert's exposition was clearly incomplete. It is, therefore, not surprising that the *incipit* to the Prologue of the Balliol manuscript makes it clear that John was writing *super extremam partem cantici canticorum, ab eo loco, 'Dilectus meus candidus et rubicundus'*.[48] Certainly he was quite aware of what he was taking on, even though in his prologue he expressed his aims very modestly.[49] I think it scarcely conceivable that he tried his hand without some form of encouragement from either the General Chapter, or, say, the abbot of Cîteaux. Such encouragement has left absolutely no record behind it, as far as we know, and the fact that he finished the job also left no mark. These two things could very easily have some connection with the times in which he was bringing his commentary together. When was this?

References in Sermons 41 and 76 to political affairs during the Interdict, make it clear that a crucial stage in this process was reached in 1210.[50] My own guess is that he pondered the theme for a very much longer period than the last few years of his life, just as Saint Bernard had done. There is at least one indication within the finished commentary that notes used during actual preaching were worked up into the literary form of sermons.[51] But in any case the time when he seems to have been bringing his thoughts to a conclusion coincided with the most stressful time of his life, when, indeed,

---

48. Cant Serm. p. 33.
49. The passage is quoted by Bell, page 148 below.
50. Cant Serm, xiii.
51. Cant Serm 8.4; p. 81, 79; marginal note: 'Haec post editum sermonem in schedule interposuit satisfactorium quibus de modi super hoc dicto uidelicet Iesum haereditarium a matre uirgine accepisse innocentiam'. Beckett did not translate this; ET 1:164.

Fig. 6   Pillar on south side of chapter house.

Fig. 7 Detail of same chapter house pillar.

Forde was reduced by royal demands for money to a new poverty, being forced to sell much of its moveable wealth.[52] Stress coincided with old age, for if we are right in supposing that John entered Forde around 1169, then it is likely that he was born before 1154, since, according to the Order's regulations, he should not have been admitted as a novice until he was fifteen.[53] So, by 1210 he was approaching sixty, then considered really old (though now we think of it as the beginning of man or woman's third age).

Surely, then, it is not strange that his final work contained so many references to the pulls which he felt between his duties to his community and to himself, or between the duties which took him away from Forde and his desire to be at peace at home. Let me quote a passage, from Sermon 117:

> Would that your peace would rest upon us, the servant of your peace, from whose disturbance and hastening to and fro you reap this peace! Would that when we return to you soaked to the skin, abused on all sides, completely exhausted from the contentions of the market-place, we should gain warmth and find concealment among you from the storm and the flood![54]

John's experience out in the world, as well as in the monastery— which he saw sometimes with very acute eyes—deeply coloured the pages of his greatest work, whose true significance in the life of its day we are only now beginning to see. Maybe we can suggest that one of the things which not merely formed him as a writer, but even induced him to put pen to parchment, or stylus to wax tablets, was the frequency with which he was out in the world which originally he had hoped to leave. John may have been made a writer, not

52. Cant Serm 76.9; pp. 532–533.
53. Canivez, *Statuta* 1:31.
54. Cant Serm 117.12; p. 794, 259–264 (my translation). Cf. Cant Serm 7; p. 216. The commentary has much to say on the stresses between the duties of the pastor and his desire to pray, action and contemplation, Martha and Mary, which has not yet been thoroughly explored.

just by belonging to a community where books and other writers existed, but because he needed to give written form to his spiritual teaching so that the monks, from whom he was so often absent, could read and digest the kernel of his ideas. Other more stationary abbots, stay-at-homes, did not have the same urge to undertake what for any author at any time is a perilous and alarming test, that of giving permanent form to thoughts, which if not written down can be revised again and again as they are spoken.[55] Most abbots could fulfil their task of forming their monks along the ways indicated by the Gospel and Saint Benedict without ever engaging in the curious art of writing: John could not, perhaps because he was on the road so often. And to that repeated circumstance we may owe the existence of this book and the colloquium upon which it is based.

In this generation I suspect that John's works will attract rather diverse readers. Those looking for evidence of the outer life of the time may turn first to the *Life of Wulfric*, whilst those interested in the spirituality may go to the sermon-commentary, even though, as Pauline Matarasso and Marsha Dutton show, the *Life* is deeply imbued with the same spirituality to be found in the sermons. For me, once I have accustomed myself to John's almost Schubertian length (if one may use a parallel from music), the Commentary really engages me when he speaks of his own experience and reveals the quality of his concern for his monks. He may not describe them with the verve which Aelred does, but they emerge as a human and fallible audience. As far as we know now, those pictures were not enjoyed by many of his contemporaries, or indeed by many later readers, until this present generation. Perhaps they, like some of us, found him too longwinded, and, as David Bell has shown very clearly, his approach to exegesis was out of step with the new ways of the schools. Not all who now can value him will be troubled by his 'old-fashioned' guise, however, since for them he still seems a guide to inward exploration where presence, renewal and love can be found.

---

55. I originally made this suggestion in Christopher Holdsworth, 'Frühe zisterziensiche Spiritualität in Forde', in *Die Zisterzienser: Ordensleben zwischen Ideal und Wirklichkeit*, edd. Kaspar Elm and Peter Joerissen (Cologne, 1982) 67–68.

Pauline Matarasso _____

John Of Forde as Portrait Painter
In The *Vita Beati Wulfrici*

A TRANSLATOR spends a lot of time with a text and time is an important factor in forming friendships; but time alone is not enough. I should like to introduce you to some friends I made while I was engaged in translating. In no other medieval text, Latin or French, have I met characters that have come alive for me as have those who inhabit the pages of John of Forde's *Life of Wulfric of Haselbury*. So vivid have one or two become that I fancy I know what they look like. Colin Morris, defining what we mean today by a portrait, wrote: 'You would know the subject if you saw him in his bath'[1]—without, that is, his hauberk, habit, mitre, orb and sceptre, or indeed his city suit. I feel that I should know Wulfric in his bath—his cold bath, of course. This led me to ask myself what it was that distinguished this work from so many others and what it tells us about John of Forde as a writer and a human being. So that we may approach John's portrait gallery with a little more understanding of what he has achieved, I should like to take a brief look at the wider context.

We might usefully start by noting some differences between the mediæval and modern concepts of selfhood. We lay great stress today on the individual. People see themselves as individuals distinct from society, against which they define themselves and from which

1. *The Discovery of the Individual, 1050–1200*, (London: SPCK 1972) p. 87.

they frequently seek differentiation. To speak of a person, an idea or a work as 'highly individual' is to pay a notable compliment, whereas 'running with the herd', although it is in fact what most of us do most of the time, is seen as somewhat contemptible. For medieval man this was not so; his ambition was to pattern himself on the norm—or possibly, for the zealous, to surpass it in reaching out to the ideal. A knight achieved renown by excelling in certain qualities that were required for all: strength, athleticism, courage, prudence, counsel. For the monk the situation was at once more complex and more circumscribed. The pressure to conform was still greater because his community was more cohesive, his way of life more formalised. At the same time he was required to excel in just those virtues which contradict the very notion of excelling: humility, self-abasement, love. A monk might be first in the eyes of others, but only on condition of being last in his own. The nobility can be said, very loosely, to have had a common ideal, to which many paid only lip-service. The religious were more constrained: they had a common rule to which they were bound by vow, and the very fact that it was a shared observance set it above any individual striving for perfection. Hence we have Saint Bernard leaving off his hair-shirt in his later years in order to return to the norm, to be one with the brothers.[2]

The medieval perception of selfhood was a product of processes of history and culture too complex to examine. But I would suggest that, particularly in the cloister, it was reinforced by the doctrine of the *imago Dei* which was so central to monastic theology. For if we were all created in God's image and lost that likeness through sin, then the whole trend of our lives should be a reversion to type, what cistercian writers, following Saint Paul, refer to as being conformed to Christ; and if that does not preclude individual variations and differences, since any number of variants can be contained in the oneness of God, it does put our 'individuality' as opposed to our selfhood into perspective.

Given the different understanding of the relationship between self and society, it is not surprising that when we look for lifelike

2. Geoffrey of Auxerre, *Vita Prima*, III.i.1; PL 185:304.

portraits in mediæval literature we find a desert inhabited by wraiths. They are all see-through people. Take that hall of mirrors in which chivalry liked to see itself reflected: the arthurian romances. The knights of the Round Table are walking variations on a theme: the courtly Gawain, the abrupt Kay, the innocent Perceval, and so on. One writer steeped in cistercian spirituality had no difficulty in using them as pegs on which to hang an allegorical interpretation having all its references in Scripture and the Fathers. Gawain became a kind of mediæval Mr Wordly-wiseman, Lancelot symbolised Adam or Everyman, Perceval and Bors, grace and works, and Galahad was of course a figure of Christ.[3]

If one looks at what purports to be a biography, the picture is much the same. Only the holy qualified for what we would recognize as *Lives*. The great of the world were commemorated in chronicle or epic, the emphasis in both being on deeds. The saint, on the other hand, was his deed—Malachy was his own greatest miracle, according to Bernard—so some attention was focused on his being, as opposed to his doing.[4] But here too, indeed here particularly, the norm operated. There was a procrustean bed on which saints were laid, and if they did not fit, adjustments were made, not to the bed but to the saint, and in the process any traits which today we would consider individual tended to be eliminated, either because they were thought to spoil the fit, or simply because they were not of interest. They were not what made a man holy, and his holiness was the only significant thing about him, because it reflected the unknowable and unseeable God.

Saints' lives were usually written by their disciples, and a close friend can act as a window, allowing something of the personality to shine through. But medieval glass can be very opaque, Geoffrey of Auxerre can hardly be said to mediate Bernard's personality. William of Saint Thierry has more insight, but looking at Bernard through

---

3. *La Queste del Saint Graal*, ed. A. Pauphilet, CFMA, Paris 1923, reprinted 1949. For the cistercian background to this work, see Matarasso, *The Redemption of Chivalry: A Study of the 'Queste del Saint Graal'* (Geneva: Droz, 1979).
4. VMal., xix. 43 (SBOp 3:348).

William is very much like looking at the altar through a squint. Bernard himself was a very indifferent biographer. One suspects that he did not really see other people; he saw only Christ in them. It is true that his acquaintance with Malachy was brief, but the life he wrote could be described as rhetoric draped over a cardboard cutout. He was delineating not a man, but his vision of the ideal pastor. The author of the Life of Godschalk, finding that Malachy's clothes fitted his own saint to a tee and were beautifully embroidered into the bargain, had no hesitation in borrowing from Saint Bernard what he needed.[5] In an age that perceived the holy as coming in a very few stock shapes and sizes, saints could be easily dressed off the peg.

Walter Daniel, who wrote the life of Aelred, is a happy exception.[6] If he was indeed the infirmarer of Rievaulx it would explain his unusual interest in the physical. It is true that he fails to tell us whether Aelred was tall or short, dark or fair, but the abbot is none the less for Walter a specific bodily presence: frail, gaunt, in frequent pain, sitting on a mat beside the fire trying to rub a little warmth into arthritic limbs. A saint he may have been; for Walter he was also a man whom he had nursed and over whom he watched jealously like an incorruptible and rather snappy sheepdog. And Aelred's holiness comes over more strongly because, thanks to Walter, we can embrace him as a man. Just as God's love became incarnate in Christ so that we might better grasp it, so holiness is perceived as more real, more lovable, more holy in men and women with whose humanity we can identify. But in the Middle Ages people obviously felt otherwise: they liked their saints to be apart, hieratic like the portrayals of Christ in majesty.

This is a very superficial survey of the scene, but it can serve as a backcloth against which to set John's Life of Wulfric. Wulfric of Haselbury was born in Somerset in the late eleventh century. After a period as parish priest of his native village, he spent the last thirty years of his life in a cell built onto the church of Saint Michael at

5. Cf. SBOp. 3:348, note 12.
6. Vita Ailredi, critical edition and translation by F. M. Powicke (London: Nelson, 1950; translation rpt. Kalamazoo, 1994).

Haselbury Plucknett, a few miles from Forde. There he died in 1154. During his lifetime his fame as a prophet and miracle worker spread well beyond the locality, he was visited by kings and princes, and people came to see him from as far afield as Kent and Yorkshire. Yet after his death a great silence descended. A dispute over his body arose between the monks of Montacute, who had furnished his daily pittance, and the villagers of Haselbury, and the latter, thanks to the resourcefulness of the parish priest, won the day. But the villagers were unable to exploit their victory as the monks would have done. The anchorite's grave remained unmarked, its place, for fear of monkish body-snatchers, known only to God and Osbern the priest, and thirty years after Wulfric's death John could write sadly, 'it is as though he had never been'.[7]

The source of John's interest in Wulfric seems to have lain in tales told in the cloister. It is true that in his prefatory letters he claims to have received the encouragement of both abbot and bishop, but he was bound to seek their approval for his work and present it as elicited by them. It seems likely, if only from the time-span involved, that his was the initial interest, theirs the authority under which it took written form. Certainly there were a number of monks at Forde, when John entered, who had known Wulfric; two, at least, were still alive in the 1180s. John seems to have found their stories so compelling that he wanted to know more. One might say that he got hooked on Wulfric. Undoubtedly the miraculous element was a powerful draw. Who could resist tales of rings plucked from a mail shirt in a kind of spiritual conjuring trick? Not Brother William the guest master, who had seen it done many times and was not above provoking a repetition, nor John who plainly wished he had been there too.[8] But I think that John was also attracted by Wulfric's personality and that the stories furnished him with a thread that he had to follow back to its beginning. We know that his interest in the holy man developed over a number of years, for some of the people who gave him information were dead by the time he wrote.[9]

7. Wulf, Prologue; p. 7.
8. Wulf 72; pp. 100–101.
9. See the discussion by Bell in Wulf, pp. xx-xxxix.

This slow maturation allowed time for Wulfric to grow in John and explains in part how he emerged so fully rounded in the *Life*. It also shows a doggedness in John; he did not give up or let go, and this same quality is evident in his conscientious ferreting out of facts and checking of informants.

When John of Forde embarked on his *Life of Wulfric* he disposed in one chapter of the saint's first thirty or forty years, which, since he was not yet holy, were of no significance. Thereafter there were no events, so individual chapters, each encapsulating one anecdote, could be strung together like so many rosary beads. Some chapters, and not the least interesting, are wholly given over to one man of God reflecting on another. John had to dig deep into his own spirituality to comprehend Wulfric's. Chapter Two, entitled The Grace of the Inner Man, is a meditation in which John draws equally on the riches of his own spiritual life and on his long frequentation of Wulfric to come to some approximation of Wulfric's inner life after his enclosure. He concludes with a definition of his aim: 'I have touched on, rather than exhausted, what is personal and inward, and that only insofar as an outsider may properly look into the holy of holies . . . . My part in rendering homage to the man is to give a faithful account of all that was admirable in his outward being and doing, both initially and as he progressed.'[10]

There are two or three points to comment on. First, John does not, in fact, confine himself to Wulfric's outward being and doing. He is too involved and too deeply human to leave it at that. He is always intervening to explain Wulfric to the reader, to examine what we should call his psychology, to set what might seem strange or outlandish in context. In fact, he records aspects of Wulfric's character that clearly puzzle him and that he does not find immediately

10. Wulf, 2; 16–17. Cf. William of Saint Thierry on Bernard, *Vita Prima*, I. pref. (PL 185:226): 'nequaquam totam vitam Viri Dei suscepi digerendam, sed ex parte . . . opera quaedam exterioris cum hominibus conversationis ejus . . . non invisibilem illam vitam viventis et loquentis in eo Christi ennarrare proposui, sed exteriora quaedam vitae ipsius experimenta, de puritate interioris sanctitatis et invisibilis conscientiae, per opera exterioris hominis, ad sensus hominis exteriores micantia.'

admirable, aspects that he is at great pains to reflect on, often in depth, and integrate with what he has come to know of Wulfric and his life. This in turn leads us to the 'faithfulness' which he proposes to bring to his account. One can only say that he has admirably fulfilled his promise. Not only does he include anecdotes that perplex him and that he fears might tell against the saint, he is scrupulous in advancing nothing that is not vouched for by one or more trustworthy witnesses.

It is worth pausing a moment to examine John of Forde's concern to get at the facts, to report only what happened—what I would call a concern for accuracy rather than truth. Truth comes in many guises. I have always thought it was Pilate's misfortune to say 'What is truth?' at the wrong moment. At any other time it would have been a perfectly legitimate question. The twelfth-century writer of the *Liber visionum et miraculorum* compiled at Clairvaux was much more easy-going than John of Forde. He accepted that some of the stories lack what he calls the testimony of certitude, but he justifies their inclusion on the grounds that they can still arouse in the reader a sense of devotion which is itself a 'true' feeling and tending to the truth. He further asserts that 'just as what is false has no foundation in certitude, so many things that are uncertain have beneath them a foundation of truth'.[11] John of Forde would never have used such an argument. He was far more rigorous. He always gives the name of the person from whom he heard the story and he takes pains to establish his or her credibility: at the very least the named person is 'well respected and religious'. Unless he has complete confidence in the reliability of the witness—as, for example, Brother William, with whom he had lived for many years at Forde—he prefers to double check. On one occasion he went even further: 'Because,' he writes, 'I did not hear this story myself, and because the woman lives not far from the monastery, I sent three of the most trustworthy brothers individually to her.'[12] Again, when relating one of Wulfric's

11. See Brian Patrick McGuire, 'A Lost Clairvaux Exemplum Collection Found: the "Liber Visionum et Miraculorum", compiled under prior John of Clairvaux', *Analecta Cisterciensia* 39, 1983, pp. 27–62, espec. at p. 33.
12. Wulf, 105; p.132.

best known and one could almost say most popular miracles, John writes:

> So much I had from Brother William, the guestmaster of Ford, and Dom Walter, monk of Glastonbury, not to mention others whom it would take too long to name. Some give varying accounts of the cutting of the hauberk and other details, but differences are merely circumstantial. I think, however, that I have learned the truth after long scrutiny and by relying on what I believe to be the more dependable testimony of proven honesty and age.[13]

Walter of Glastonbury, mentioned there, was one of John's most fecund sources of information.[14] He was the son of William fitzWalter, the local lord who was Wulfric's protector and patron. Wulfric served for years as the family's holy man and friend, the repository of hopes and sorrows and secrets, consulted and dropped in on by all its members. Walter is therefore well vouched for; but this is not enough for John. 'It is time,' he writes towards the end of his book, 'that I myself bore witness to my witness and spared a few words to establish his credentials.'[15] In fact, he spares a good many, and finally, having accompanied Walter to his establishment as a black monk at Glastonbury, he concludes the chapter with these revealing comments:

> He has lived there ever since, giving no occasion for complaint, held in high favour, and has now attained a ripe old age. He is prepared to give an account of blessed Wulfric's life to all who ask—at a suitable time—and both his religious profession and his age preserve him from any suspicion of untruth. Any good and simple man is ashamed to lie; in a monk such a thing is totally unbecoming. Further, it is deceitful, wicked and altogether abominable for a witness to

13. Wulf, 10; p. 24.
14. Wulf, pp. xx-xxii.
15. Wulf, 96; p. 120.

the truth, when his testimony is brought forward publicly, to side with falsehood and uphold a lie. And lastly, to see a white-haired ancient cutting japes and playing the fool is unpleasant enough; but for such a one, on the very threshold of eternity, to spend his time concocting idle tales is not merely unattractive, it must appear thoroughly repellent.[16]

I think it quite safe to say on the evidence that John believed that everything he recorded in his book had taken place, that he was neither foolish nor credulous, and that he had, in fact, used every means at his disposal to verify Wulfric's claim to holiness. This is not to say that modern knowledge would not sometimes lead to different interpretations of the evidence. But John was honest, and within the limitations of his time he sifted intelligently and reported accurately what he was told. It is important to establish both John's *bona fides* and his competence before assessing his skill as a portrait painter. We have to know how important it was to him to achieve a likeness. Clearly to Saint Bernard it mattered not a lot.

In his *Life of Wulfric* John opens for us a window on to a peopled landscape. He affords us a rare look at the world outside the cloister and it is refreshing to find that he considers it of value. There are no expressions of contempt, or even of monastic superiority, and he plainly thinks that his cast of characters were living worthwhile lives. Wulfric is at the heart of the book, and he also seems to have been at the heart of the village, the magnet which drew the community together and exerted a powerful pull over a wide area round, and wherever word of him spread, along invisible lines of communication which stretched to the king's court and even beyond the sea. The community consisted of the lord, William fitzWalter— not always in residence for he had other manors, his wife Beatrix, his children and household (notably his bailiff), the parish priest Brichtric, who was married and was in due course succeeded by his son Osbern, and the mostly unnamed villagers. All these had Wulfric's ear and for all he showed concern, refusing once to speak

16. Wulf, 96; p. 122.

to a visitor until he had gone back and helped free a cart stuck in the mud which he had ignored in passing.[17] A wider circle drawn round Haselbury would take in a vassal of William fitzWalter who was fond of fishing, three priests, an anchoress at Crewkerne, one or maybe two successive anchoresses of Wareham, a number of local notables, and of course the anonymous crowd of those whom John calls the pious people of the district.

Within the same circle lay two abbeys: Montacute and Forde. Relations with Montacute were somewhat strained; there was an arrangement whereby the community furnished Wulfric with his daily bread, but the bursar made constant difficulties, until an exasperated and no doubt hungry Wulfric one day invoked God's wrath on the man with terrible results.[18] What with that, and the abbey's failure to secure his body, a certain ambivalence towards Wulfric's memory could be expected at Montacute and John does not cite any tales emanating from that source. Forde, on the other hand, was a rich repository of Wulfriciana.[19] There was Richard the cantor, who had once been Wulfric's scribe, his three brothers and his son. Richard's father, Segar, was a priest who was at one time living at Haselbury. Richard and Segar both knew Wulfric well. There were a number of monks who came to John with tales from their own villages, but most importantly there were two brothers, a certain John and, more particularly, William the guestmaster, who had been close friends of the recluse and had both known the long dead Brichtric. William, certainly, was still alive in 1184.

A family of great nobles with local connections were frequent visitors. Bence, wife of Robert of Lincoln, and her son Alfred turned up regularly in Haselbury and were once fed, together with their considerable escort, with one loaf and no fishes. Alfred's uncle, Samson of Lincoln, was the brother of lady FitzWalter, and was cured of a fever by Wulfric.[20] Henry I called by in state when on a visit to Wessex. A certain Drogo de Munci had suffered a stroke

17. Wulf, 70; p. 97.
18. Wulf, 45; pp. 61–3.
19. Wulf, pp. xxii-xxvi.
20. Wulf, 66; p. 94 and 41, pp. 57–8, 154–5.

at court after calling Wulfric a charlatan and accusing him of sharp practice and money hoarding. The king, pressed by the queen, went to the saint to seek a cure for Drogo. Wulfric obliged, without any enthusiasm, it must be said, allowing his hand to be placed on the sick man's twisted face.[21] Stephen of Blois went to Haselbury at least twice, before and again after his accession to the throne. Wulfric was no respecter of persons: on one occasion he took Stephen so severely to task about some hidden sin that the king, weeping, presented his cheek to the prophet to be struck and spat upon.[22] I see no reason to believe that Wulfric held back.

Such were the men and women of all conditions who came on foot, on horseback, or in litters to Wulfric's cell at Haselbury for the thirty years he occupied it. The great majority are bit players in John's book; they come on, act out their dumb show and depart. But some appear several times and in a variety of circumstances, and this in itself works powerfully in their favour, for each time they resurface after an interval one has a sense of *déjà vu*, until it becomes a matter of greeting an old friend. At the same time each new anecdote lights them from a different angle, giving an impression of solidity. Furthermore, the anecdotes are, despite the miraculous element, very firmly rooted in the soil of daily life. Food, for example—despite, or perhaps because of Wulfric's austerities— bulks very large, whether it is food sent to him, food refused him, food from heaven, food multiplied, food shared with friends, or food stolen from him which turns to stone or becomes infested with maggots.[23] Wulfric assures the bailiff that his master will arrive early the following morning and he had better have a good meal

21. Wulf, 46; pp. 63–5. Drogo witnesses *acta* of Henry I 15 times: 1110– 34: *Regesta Regum Anglo-Normannorum 1066–1154*, vol II. *1100–1135*, edd. C. Johnson and H. A. Cronne (Oxford 1956), nos. 956, 1246, 1303, 1325, 1366, 1418, 1556, 1596, 1719, 1724, 1827, 1862–3, 1900–01. He is not mentioned by Judith A. Green, *The Government of England under Henry I* (Cambridge 1956).

22. Wulf, 91; pp. 117–18: cf. Ch. 7, p. 21.

23. Wulf, 40 (from heaven), 41 (multiplied), 37, 72 (shared with friends), 43, 84 (stolen and transformed); pp. 56–7, 57–8, 54–5, 99–100, 59–60, 110–111.

ready. When the bailiff expresses doubt, Wulfric insists: the master is having his horses foddered this very minute.[24]

In consequence, all these people can be seen in their habitual occupations. When Brichtric is not about his parish duties he spends his time in the church, praying and reciting the psalms. He goes home to dinner, but on horseback, so as to waste no time getting back. Like Wulfric, he is a very believable combination of the holy and the human. The two men were normally, says John, like a pair of turtle doves, but they managed to fall out over a miracle. Wulfric loosed the tongue of a dumb man who then revealed himself fluent not only in English but in French. Brichtric took the huff: 'Look,' he said, 'I've served you for years and all for nothing. You've never enabled me to speak French, and when I come before the bishop and the archdeacon I have to stand as dumb as any mute.'[25] Wulfric thought it a great joke and related the story to brother William.

Wulfric's cell was on the north side of the church and he felt the cold, so when a mouse nibbled his new cape he was not pleased. 'Perish that mouse!' he exclaimed in a moment of exasperation and was horrified when it did just that. He promptly sent for Brichtric and confessed what he had done. 'If only you would dispatch all the local mice in the same way,' said the priest unfeelingly. 'God forbid!' said Wulfric, 'Once, with one mouse, was a very grave fault, and, if I didn't think it would displease my Lord, I would pray to him to bring this mouse to life again.'[26]

John shared his hero's breadth of sympathy, if not with the animal world, at least with all sorts and conditions of men. Anyone able to flesh out his picture of Wulfric was welcome in John's book. Women in particular found an open door. Besides two queens, four or five noblewomen and three anchoresses, there is a significant company of nameless women who came to Wulfric, sent him presents, cooked for him, and in return received his wisdom, his blessing, his prayers, and sometimes a cure for their ailments.

24. Wulf, 94; pp. 119–20.
25. Wulf, 14; p. 29.
26. Wulf, 30; p. 47.

John devotes an unusual amount of space to Matilda, an anchoress of Wareham whom Wulfric directed when she came to him in search of her vocation.[27] John had his information from Christina, the recluse who followed Gertrude, Matilda's servant and her immediate successor in the cell. Despite John's hard work on behalf of Matilda, I must admit that she remains faceless for me; perhaps because what John most admired was the holy silence in which she suffered the agonies of toothache until the tooth and a bit of rotted bone fell out and were discreetly hidden behind a loose stone in the wall, to be discovered after her death by the faithful Gertrude, who had, when clutching her own jaw, been chided by Matilda for complaining. These pages are very much the stock in trade of hagiography. John is always better when forced to leave this well-beaten path and explore rougher countryside. Lady fitzWalter's memory is preserved by the cruel snub administered to her by the queen. Riding home from Corfe castle to Haselbury, she took her shame and anger straight to Wulfric, whom she loved for his *sanctitas* and *suavitas*, and he did not find it beneath his holiness to comfort her for this social humiliation, nor did John scruple to recount it.[28] To them it was just a part of life, but for us a part that rarely gets chronicled.

John gives us too perhaps the only glimpse of a real twelfth-century boy. Osbern, who was to succeed his father Brichtic as parish priest of Haselbury, acted as Mass server and acolyte to both his father and the anchorite. One Sunday morning when Brichtric wanted to bless the water in the church, Osbern suddenly realised that he had taken the *aspersorium* home and left it there. What would his father say? Quick! he thought, I'll borrow the holy man's. But when he opened the door of the cell he found Wulfric gazing fixedly at a bright light over the altar. Osbern was so fascinated that he thrust the *aspersorium* at someone else to give to the priest, and, having quietly pushed the cell door to, he applied one eye to the crack and watched what was happening inside, thereby providing

27. Wulf, 56–7; pp. 81–5.
28. Wulf, 81; pp. 108–9.

posterity, unwittingly, with the internal geography of the cell. It is a wonderfully boyish reaction and it lives and sparkles in John's words, which are surely those in which Osbern, many years later, related it to him.[29]

On another occasion Wulfric had an intuition that a visitor was coming to assist at his Mass. He kept an increasingly frustrated Osbern hanging around for what seemed like hours when he would far sooner have been playing. At last a monk hove in sight, to be met by Osbern in the churchyard with the words: 'We've waited for you all this time, and very boring it has been, too.'[30] This makes a refreshing change from the usual banalities of the genre. Jocelyn of Furness, in his Life of Waltheof, shows the future saint lisping his childish way through the Mass in a pretend church while his brother Simon plays at besieging mock castles.[31] It seems a pretty enough picture until one realizes that each is merely shown as acting out the well worn hagiographical cliché of the boy being father to the man.

In all these anecdotes John of Forde's dialogue is wonderful. It is always totally convincing and does more than anything else to bring his characters to life. Here is Wulfric again with Osbern, grown up now and parish priest:

'Osbern, isn't this the candle you gave me yesterday evening?'

'It certainly is.'

'And isn't it still as big as it was?'

'I can see that it is indeed as big and I am amazed.'

'Three times I said my night office by its light, and you see what my Lord did for me.'

'What can I say, save that it seems to be a kind of joke on the part of the divine majesty.'

'Thanks be to him; he is my Lord; let him do as he wants with his servant.'[32]

I do not think that John of Forde was 'good at dialogue' in the way one might say that of a novelist. In fact, I think his powers of

29. Wulf, 35; pp. 52–53.
30. Wulf, 74; pp. 102–103.
31. *Vita S. Waldoni*, Acta SS., iii Aug: c. 249.
32. Wulf, 34; p. 51.

imagination were slight, which is probably a blessing. I believe that Wulfric's *ipsissima verba* were passed down in the bare and rather lapidary English that he spoke (John says at one point that he was a man of few words),[33] and that John rendered them into Latin as faithfully as they had been passed from mouth to mouth. It is all of a piece with his concern for accuracy. He was a natural reporter, and he was also aware that direct speech is a great enlivener, for when he came to one of his longest stories he put it all in the first person.

Henry, abbot of Tintern and Waverley, had in his youth contributed in no small way to the anarchy under Stephen. He owed his conversion to Wulfric and he told the whole story to the abbot of Forde and to John himself as the three men travelled together to a meeting of the General Chapter. That John had a retentive ear and an uncumbered memory in which to store what he heard is evident from the opening sentence:

> I am familiar with every detail of the story, for I heard it myself from his own lips, as though God had chosen me in advance as a witness fit and able to transmit it all to you. I shall tell the tale in his own words to give it a livelier pace.[34]

The words John goes on to put in the mouth of Father Henry are in fact very different in style from the dialogue that emanates from Wulfric's cell. Father Henry, although delightful, is somewhat orotund, not unlike John, and salts his narrative liberally with quotations from Scripture. It is my guess that the story was first related, at least in part, in Latin. And if it seems strange that two abbots and a monk, all three of them English—because the abbot of Forde was almost certainly Baldwin—should speak Latin together on a long and tedious journey, I can but call to mind that Baldwin preached the Crusade in Latin round the castles and villages of Wales, where, according to Gerald who accompanied him, they were all moved to tears by his eloquence. Perhaps he had expressive body

33. Wulf, 8; p. 21.
34. Wulf, 50; p. 68.

language. Certainly when Father Henry recounts his conversations with Wulfric he reverts to the simple, pithy phrases that John always puts in Wulfric's mouth.

Father Henry is delightful because he lays himself open to our gaze without any reticence, but also with complete lack of self-regard. He did not expect to find himself in a book. He had touching little vanities which were always being punctured by Wulfric. After an initial conversion he backslid, and had to go through it all again, more painfully, before he was finally tossed up safe on the shore at Waverley. Anxious to let Wulfric know that his prophecies had been fulfilled, he found an excuse to go to Haselbury.

> 'I will go,' he said, 'and see the man of God and congratulate him on his accuracy in my regard, and tell him that not one of all his words has failed of its promise. And indeed, if he promised me so many good things when I was an enemy still and a traitor, what will he not announce to me now that I am reconciled? And should there be miracles—who knows? for me to work, he would certainly not keep it to himself.'[35]

Splendidly complacent he hurried in to Wulfric and greeted him with the words: 'Master, I am that man to whom you once foretold things which now, by God's grace, are fulfilled in me. Here before you see the fruits of your prophecy. I have therefore come back to you to enable you to give thanks to God, who has had mercy on me and proved you truthful as well' Back came this medicinal word: 'Quite so, my son; keep the rule of your order and you will be able to save your soul.' Father Henry admitted to instant deflation.[36]

So devoted to Wulfric's cause was Father Henry ever afterwards that on all his journeyings he carried Wulfric's name about with him as, said John, a lutanist does his lute. Like a Welsh bard 'harping on' he no doubt bored many on the way. In fact, it was possible to

35. Wulf, 50; p. 71.
36. Wulf, 50; p. 72: 'Statim detumui fateor . . . .'

measure the holiness of his hearers by the way they responded. Yet Father Henry had his great day:

> When at last he obtained an audience with the pope he duly produced his Wulfric, and although he spoke passionately and at length he could not say enough for the pontiff, who proved a no less passionate listener. During this time there were great men waiting outside, pillars of the Church anxious to gain access but unable, and matters of vast importance and the business of all the lands of christendom requiring the pope's attention were left in suspense. The lord pope meanwhile and Father Henry were within, foregathered in Wulfric's name. Wholly occupied with the mystery of holiness, they were eating their honeycomb with their honey and drinking their wine with their milk. And Father Henry, as he told us later, was secretly glorying in the fact that he had all to himself the attention of the man whom all the world waited on, and was seen to enjoy not only the right of access to such greatness, but even a certain intimacy and fellowship.[37]

Let me say, in case you get too exclusively human an impression of Father Henry, that John is eloquent on the subject of his holiness and austerity of life. His sound administration also pulled the community at Tintern back from the brink.

Father Henry's devotion to Wulfric must have been to John like a seal of approval. Here was a man of noble birth, of some education certainly, who had risen with exceptional speed from novice to abbot, who was widely respected if not revered, yet who enthusiastically endorsed the claim to sanctity of a man in many ways his opposite. For Wulfric was neither well born nor highly educated, and over the years he had acquired certain eccentricities. John, who was cast much more in the mould of Father Henry than of Wulfric and who had not the advantage of personal acquaintance,

37. Wulf, 52; p. 76.

had to make a great imaginative leap, not only to encompass Wulfric, but also to present him to the reader. When John seeks to render the essence of Wulfric, the term of his choice is *simplicitas*. 'Simplicity,' he says, 'complemented and refined his faith, overlaying it with pure gold. It was an inborn thing, but by the sanctifying power of the Holy Spirit the gift of nature had become a gift of grace.'[38] John was always being brought up short by Wulfric's simplicity. He discerned it in the story of the mouse: 'That most simple of men was more humbled than otherwise by this sign.' And again: 'Such was the man, a marvellous combination of greatness and simplicity!'[39] He frequently comments on the simplicity of the answers Wulfric gave to people, and one is indeed put in mind of Joan of Arc's replies to her judges. 'His words,' says John, 'were like loaves fresh from the oven and gave off a wonderful scent of purity and simplicity of heart.'[40] He sees the same simplicity at work in Wulfric's relations with his visitors. No-one was deferred to, no-one was gratified with a title. Even Saint Bernard got short shrift when he referred to Wulfric via Father Henry a matter that was troubling his conscience.[41] Similarly, when recounting how Wulfric sent on his deathbed for the bishop of Bath and gave him strict instructions about his burial, John comments: 'This was neither an entreaty nor the anxiety of a self-important man to procure in advance the ministrations of the great at his funeral rites. Frank and free in his simplicity, he enjoined even on the bishop what he foresaw in spirit should and ought to be done.'[42]

In John's eyes a native artlessness in Wulfric had become a *sancta simplicitas*. There were, of course, those who saw it otherwise. A certain monk of Forde, whom John was too discreet to name,

38. Wulf, 2; p. 16.
39. Wulf, 30; p. 46–47.
40. Wulf, 7; p. 20. Saint Bernard used the same image, not here as a simile, but as a metaphor: 'O quam libens pariter tibi calidos panes, quos utique adhuc fumigantes, et quasi modo de furno tractos, ut aiunt, recens tractos, de caelesti largitate crebro Christus suis pauperibus frangit.' Ep. 106 to Henry Murdac (SBOp 7:266).
41. Wulf, 54; p. 79.
42. Wulf, 99; p. 125.

snorted with disbelief over Wulfric's claim to concentrate with perfect single-mindedness throughout the recitation of the psalter. Simple people, he maintained, had fewer powers of concentration, and it was only Wulfric's lack of intellectual range that led him to make such claims: he did not know what concentration meant. Needless to say, the monk got his come-uppance, though of a very blessed kind.[43]

Simplicity lay, for John, at the heart of the man, and he used it as the key to unlock a major difficulty in which he found himself boxed. John, as we have see, was very scrupulous about giving the names of witnesses to the facts he alleged, but it often happened that the ultimate authority for the story was Wulfric himself. Thus we read: 'I had this from Brother William and he from the holy man.'[44] This, as John saw, raised two problems: one of authenticity, since an embarrassing number of stories would be seen to have no corroboration; and one touching Wulfric more nearly, in that blowing one's own trumpet is not a recommended exercise for a saint, and John lets it be understood that comments had been passed about Wulfric's lack of fitting discretion. His answer was to assert that Wulfric's humility went beyond the modesty that pretends it has not noticed the miracle. He would relate such things to spiritually minded people 'with a very simple smile and as though they were of no consequence at all'.[45] And in fact, to Wulfric, they were not. This at least is the conclusion that John came to after long investigation. In order to give full weight to his understanding of Wulfric's simplicity he refers to the simplicity of the child, who is free to say what it wants and can walk around uncovered without being conscious of its nakedness.[46] Wulfric was such a child, with a child's directness and innocence, and this very simplicity is the best guarantee of the truth of what he said. Being what he was, he is his own best witness. The argument may appear circular, and to some degree it is, but I think that psychologically it is quite convincing.

43. Wulf, 19; pp. 36–7.
44. Wulf, 17; p. 35.
45. Wulf, 13; p. 28.
46. Wulf, 13; p. 27.

But whatever it tells us about Wulfric, it tells us more about John, about his integrity, about his concern both for factual accuracy and for spiritual truth. And this is true of the work as a whole. Every trait that John delineates, every detail that he adds to the various portraits in his Life of Wulfric, every comment on the comeliness of the characters, reflects back, to the reader, in a way of which the writer is completely unaware, his own likeness. We have already noted his anxiety to purvey nothing but the truth. We can say without fear of contradiction that he was a humorous man, because he took such pleasure in recounting Wulfric's jokes (and he was quite a tease). A humble man, who was not afraid to be present in his work, but who never obtrudes himself. An enormously generous man in all his judgments, thinking ill of none and attributing only the best motives. He refuses even to judge the monks of Montacute who were obliged to retire discomfited and mortified after the struggle for Wulfric's body: 'It is silly and ill-considered,' he writes, 'to make fun of men who have mistaken their enthusiasm for religious fervour.'[47] He mentions also the bishop, after what had clearly been a minor riot, calming the villagers down with a few well-chosen words, 'lest memories of pleasurable disorder should disturb in some degree the weaker minds'.[48] Only a man with a wonderful breadth of understanding could put it quite like that. He agonizes over two instances when harsh words of Wulfric's have dreadful consequences, and combs the Scriptures seeking light.[49] His wisdom and humanity are perhaps best illustrated in his comments on the death of the bursar of Montacute, comments which surely reveal the future abbot:

> We are on slippery ground now, where I personally watch my feet, and I would advise you to do the same in case you stumble in our present darkness. I say this to prevent any passing of premature judgment (whether to predict the man's death or the salvation of his soul when and if God

47. Wulf, 101; p. 129.
48. *Ibid.*
49. Wulf, 45 and 49; pp. 61–3, 66–8.

should so decide), and arriving at an over-hasty verdict about a death which consists at present in the destruction of the body. It is the height of blind presumption and a temptation passing human strength to seek to define what lies beyond our mortal day: matters reserved to a higher court are to be judged by God alone.[50]

We learn to love Wulfric and Father Henry because John of Forde mediates them to us. He acts as a wonderfully clear window through which we, today, see figures of another age, the ordinary and the exceptional, going about their daily lives. But all glass needs a frame and John is himself the finely wrought window frame which defines for us the space within.

---

50. Wulf, 45; p. 62. All translations are from *The Cistercian World Monastic Writings of the Twelfth Century*, trans. and ed. Pauline Matarasso (Penquin, 1993).

Marsha L. Dutton _____

John of Forde's
De Vita Beati Wulfrici Anachoretae Haselbergiae:
A Model for Cistercian Contemplative Life

IN THE LAST QUARTER of the twelfth century the cistercian abbey of Forde had a growing reputation as a center of literary activity. It is not surprising, then, that in about 1175, John, the young prior of the abbey, should have decided to test his own skills as a writer, beginning with the life of a famous local figure, the anchorite Wulfric of Haselbury.[1] Wulfric's fame throughout England and especially in the counties of Somerset and Devon meant that although the anchorite had been dead since 1154, plenty of people in the region of Forde remembered him with enough clarity to provide stories for the biographer. At the same time his death had occurred long enough earlier to make the topic a safe one: few were likely to challenge John's narrative. Unlike the immediate controversy Walter Daniel had roused in his biography of Aelred of Rievaulx a few years earlier, John's *Vita* could probably count on a casual but detached interest.

At the same time this work would allow John to try his hand at exploring some topics of special concern to twelfth-century Cistercians. This new order, founded by men committed to becoming

1. For a survey of Forde's literary tradition and a note on the date of the beginning of the *Vita Wulfrici* see Christopher Holdsworth, 'John of Ford and English Cistercian Writing 1167–1214', *Transactions of the Royal Historical Society*, 5th series, 11 (1961) 129 n. 3. See also the first paper in this present book.

'new soldiers of Christ, poor with the poor Christ',[2] found itself insistently bound up with the world of the powerful. How was it possible to live a life of contemplation in the midst of so much involvement with the world? How was it possible to pray without ceasing while administering increasingly prosperous abbeys, advising and confessing kings, interceding in affairs of Church and State? These questions, which had concerned Christians from the earliest days, now troubled Cistercians of the twelfth century, and John saw in the life of Wulfric one attempt at solution, one man's ability to combine the urgent contemplation of God with the demands of service to God's creatures. So John presented the life of this anchorite best known for his active life of counsel, prophecy, and miracles as emerging from and shaped by his unceasing search for the wisdom of God and his glimpses of that wisdom. In *De Vita Beati Wulfrici Anachoretae Haselbergiae*, John for the first time enunciated his concern with the blending of contemplation and service and so provided a model for cistercian life.

HISTORICAL BACKGROUND

The history of christian monasticism is characterized from its beginnings by tension between the eremitic and the cenobitic life. As soon as the first hermits went into the desert, disciples followed them, seeking their counsel, imitating their life, and finally forming communities around them. Often, of course, a hermit so pursued rapidly removed to a more distant spot, only to see a new community at once taking shape around him. So the desert of the ancient world bloomed with monasteries.

By the Middle Ages this pattern of human need relentlessly interrupting the solitary had become part of the essential mythology of monastic history. Athanasius reports that Antony, the fourth-century father of the desert celebrated as the patron of both anchoritic and

2. Jean de la Croix Bouton and Jean Baptiste Van Damme, eds., 'Exordium Parvum,' *Les Plus Anciens Textes de Cîteaux*, Studia et Documenta 2 (Achel: Abbaye Cistercienne, 1974) 77.

cenobitic life, began his own search for perfection by seeking out men living in solitude in order to emulate them: 'If he heard of some zealous person anywhere, he searched him out like the wise bee. He did not go back to his own place unless he had seen him, and as though receiving from him certain supplies for traveling the road to virtue, he returned.'[3] Antony's own life followed the same pattern of disciples coming to learn from the master; as Robert C. Gregg has noted: 'Antony the holy man [became] himself the destination for pilgrims and for those in need of a healer and wonder-worker.'[4]

Antony's experience was by no means unusual among the desert fathers; Peter Brown has commented that 'the lonely cells of the recluses of Egypt have been revealed, by the archæologists, to have been well furnished consulting rooms.'[5] Similarly Gregory the Great's life of Benedict of Nursia, father of western monasticism, relates the regularity with which Benedict's search for solitude was interrupted by communities desiring his leadership, a leadership for which they considered his very solitude qualified him.

As surely as the solitary was sought out and led back to life in monastic community, the monk in the early centuries of Christendom was required to exercise responsibility beyond the cloister. So Gregory himself was first drawn from the monastery to serve as deacon and then papal agent in Constantinople, then, after another five years at home in the monastery, elected to the papacy and, over his forceful protest, consecrated in 590.

The cistercian reform of the eleventh and twelfth centuries itself sought to withdraw into solitude and there discovered the inescapability of the world's call. As Jean Leclercq pointed out in a 1962 symposium on eleventh- and twelfth-century eremitism: 'The cistercian life reconciled the solitude of the desert and that "unanimity"

3. J.-P. Migne, *Patrologia Graeca* 26:844; Robert C. Gregg, trans., *Athanasius: The Life of Antony and the Letter to Marcellinus* (New York: Paulist Press, 1980) 32.

4. Gregg, p. 9.

5. 'The Rise and Function of the Holy Man in Late Antiquity', *Journal of Roman Studies* 61 (1971) 93 (reprinted in *Society and the Holy in Late Antiquity* [London and New York: Faber and Faber, 1982] 134).

in community that more than one author has lauded: each cistercian must find in the *coenobium* the "solitude of the heart" '.[6] Yet even the earliest cistercian fathers were drawn back from this claustral solitude to the restless business of the world. The active role played by Bernard is well known, as is the fact that one of his converts to cistercian life at Clairvaux became in 1145 Pope Eugene III, the first but not the last cistercian pope. In England as well Aelred of Rievaulx wrote repeated treatises of direction for Henry II both before and after his accession to the throne, Baldwin of Forde was first bishop of Worcester and then archbishop of Canterbury, and John of Forde served as confessor to King John.

The constant demands and insistent presence of the world and the call to its service were perhaps even more pronounced for medieval anchorites, those who had rejected a vocation in community in favor of lifetime enclosure but who were, because bound to their cell by a vow of stability, unable even temporarily to flee their followers. It is no wonder that works of direction for anchorites counsel strict hours of silence, with visitors turned away during those times, and dark curtains over anchorhold windows. So Aelred of Rievaulx provides a variety of warnings to the anchoress in the twelfth-century work *On Reclusion*:

> She must take care first of all that she speak rarely, then guard what she says, and finally consider to whom she speaks and in what way . . . . If someone well-known and held in high esteem—an abbot perhaps or a priest—should wish to speak to you, he should study to do so in the presence of a third person. . . . Avoid all conversation with young men or with people of doubtful character; never permit them to speak to you unless there is real need . . . . During Lent the recluse ought to maintain an unbroken silence. Since this is difficult, if not impossible, she may speak, though less often than at other times, with her confessor and

6. 'L'Eremitisme et les Cisterciens', *L'Eremitismo in Occidente nel secoli XI e XII*, Miscellanea del Centro di Studi Medioevali, IV (Milan, 1965) 573.

attendant, but to no one else unless some important visitor arrive unexpectedly from a distance.[7]

These very warnings reveal, however, that the anchorite was a captive audience, an ever-present listening ear, counselor, friend, spiritual guide, and sometimes unwilling host. To Alfwen, the *venerabili inclusa* of Flamstead, the twelfth-century Christina of Markyate turned for refuge, and Alfwen kept her there for two years.[8] Christina herself in later years was acclaimed as a holy woman, advisor to friends, family, and strangers on financial and domestic matters as well as religious ones. Thurstan of York is reported to have urged her to become superior of his foundation of Saint Clement at York,[9] and although she rejected his invitation, in time she founded her own priory, where she counseled visitors, guided callers to monastic life, and served for many years as advisor and closest friend to Geoffrey, abbot of Saint Alban's.

Similarly in the fourteenth and fifteenth centuries Julian of Norwich gained a reputation as a holy woman and a wise counselor; as such she was recommended in about 1413 to Margery Kempe by her spiritual director, an augustinian canon. Margery's report of her conversation with Julian makes it clear that Julian was well accustomed to such visits; she speaks with the quiet confidence and authority natural to one whose days are filled with just such conversations. Margery insists, in fact, that Julian is an experienced counselor for someone struggling with spiritual visitations, saying that 'the anchoress was expert in such things and could give good counsel'.[10] Margery's frequent visits to other anchorites for advice show that Julian was no anomaly.[11]

7. Inst incl 5, 7, 8; CCCM 1:641, 642, 644 (ET *Treatises I: On Jesus at the Age of Twelve, Rule for a Recluse, The Pastoral Prayer*; CF 2:50, 52, 54).

8. *The Life of Christina of Markyate: A Twelfth Century Recluse*, ed. and trans. C. H. Talbot (Oxford: Clarendon, 1959) 93–99 [hereafter Christina].

9. Christina, pp. 125–127.

10. *The Book of Margery Kempe*, ed. Sanford Brown Meech, EETS os 212 (Oxford: Oxford Univ. Press, 1940) 42.

11. Although over the past several years there has been a growing number of studies on medieval anchoritism, most scholars continue to ignore the

John of Forde's *Life of Wulfric* provides an early example of the public demands made upon someone who entered upon a solitary life of contemplation, close to the life of Christina in both date and insight into the conditions of anchoritic life, but providing much more specific and detailed evidence of the anchorite's social role. In fact, the *Vita Wulfrici* has been considered primarily as a clear example of the way in which Wulfric, and by extension all anchorites, served his community as arbitrator, wonder-worker, banker, healer, prophet, and, in the words of Peter Brown, 'hinge-man, a man who belonged to the outside world and yet could place his *dynamis,* his know-how and . . . his culture and values at the disposal of the villagers.'[12] It is in these terms and according to this model that Henry Mayr-Harting, in his 1975 article 'Functions of a Twelfth-Century Recluse', quite rightly portrayed Wulfric.[13] More recently, Christopher Holdsworth has included Wulfric's life within his valuable exploration of the lives and social roles of six twelfth- and thirteenth-century english solitaries, calling attention to the way in which their very lives of solitude, their 'liminality', shaped them as men and women of spiritual power.[14]

THE CISTERCIAN CONTEXT

As Jean Leclercq has pointed out, the early Cistercians were, despite their Order's tie to eremitic life, always of two minds about the choice they had to make between the lives of action and contemplation. So Bernard agreed to his disciple Conrad's becoming a hermit, and he suggested that monks might live in either cloister or

---

evidence for the public role of anchorites in english society. For an exception to this pattern, see Grace M. Jantzen, *Julian of Norwich: Mystic and Theologian* (London: SPCK, 1987) 28–30, and Christopher Holdsworth, n.14 below.

12. Brown, p. 86 (reprint p. 118).
13. *History* 60 (1975) 337–352.
14. 'Hermits and the Powers of the Frontier', *Saints and Saints' Lives: Essays in Honour of D. H. Farmer, Reading Medieval Studies* 16 (1990) 55–76.

hermitage: *vita continentium . . . in claustro vel in eremo.*[15] But at other times he counselled monks not to leave the community for the desert, seeing in the eremitic life only dangers and inconveniences.[16] Edmund Mikkers, speaking of 'an eremitism in Cîteaux . . . at the interior of the Order', refers to *le penchant vers la solitude* seen in cistercian authors and literature until the fourteenth century.[17]

The cistercian concern about the way in which monks of the Order, called to loving and serving God within human community, might combine the two lives appears within the earliest works of the Order and clearly shaped the young John of Forde. The importunate longing that the Fathers found in the Song of Songs for the embrace of the Bridegroom, the kiss of the lips, the sight of God's face in unending glory, shapes all their writing, and when they have the occasion to write for those of explicitly contemplative vocation, they are insistent that their audiences must leave behind the call of the world and give themselves to the love of God alone. In the epistle to the Carthusians at Mont Dieu, William of Saint-Thierry writes: 'It is for others to serve God; it is for you to cling to him. It is for others to believe in God, know him, love him, and revere him; it is for you to taste him, understand him, be acquainted with him, enjoy him.'[18] And Aelred of Rievaulx writes for another twelfth-century anchorite:

> There were two sisters, Martha and Mary. The one was busy, the other was at leisure. The one gave, the other asked. The one was anxious to serve, the other nourished her affections. . . . This is your portion, dearly beloved. Dead and buried to the world, you should be deaf to all that belongs to the world and unable to speak of it. You should not be distracted but absorbed, not emptied out but filled

15. De div 91.3; SBOp 6/1:342.
16. E.g., Circ 3.6 (SBOp 4:286–287); SC 4.4 (SBOp 2:168); for a fuller discussion see Leclercq, 570–575.
17. Response to Leclercq, following 'L'Eremitisme', 580.
18. Ep frat 1.5.15 (ET by Theodore Berkeley ocso, *The Golden Epistle*, CF 12:14).

up. Let Martha carry out her part; though it is admitted to be good, Mary's is declared better.[19]

But as only a few are actually set apart for contemplative life, the Cistercians insist that most people cannot in this life truly leave behind the life of Martha. So Bernard writes in Sermon 9 on the Song of Songs:

> What you request [the kiss of the bridegroom's lips] may delight you, but the breasts with which you may feed the little ones are better—that is, they are more essential than the wine of contemplation. It is one thing that gladdens the heart of one man and another that benefits many. For Rachel may be more beautiful, but Lia is more fruitful. Do not therefore linger in the kisses of contemplation, because better are the breasts of preaching.[20]

Aelred too, when writing for monks rather than for an anchoress, insists on the combining of contemplation and action. In a sermon for the feast of the Assumption, preaching on Luke 10:42, he notes that Mary and Martha of Bethany dwell together in the *castellum* of the Virgin, together comprising the integrated christian life:

> You see, if Mary had been alone in the house, no one would have fed the Lord; if Martha had been alone, no one would have tasted his presence and his words. Martha thus represents the action, the labor accomplished for Christ, Mary the repose that frees from bodily labor, in order to taste the sweetness of the Lord in reading, prayer, or contemplation. That is why, my brothers, so long as Christ is on earth, poor, subject to hunger, to thirst, to temptation, it is necessary that these two women inhabit the same house, that in one soul the two activities occur. . . . Do not neglect

19. Inst incl 28; CCCM 1:660 (ET CF 2:75–76).
20. SC 9.6.8; SBOp 1:47 (ET *On the Song of Songs* I, CF 4:59).

Mary for Martha, nor Martha for Mary. If you neglect Martha, who will serve Jesus? And if you neglect Mary, what will be the use of the visit of Jesus, since you will not taste his sweetness? Know, my brothers, that in this life it is necessary never to separate these two women. When the time comes that Jesus is no longer poor, no longer has hunger or thirst, is no longer tempted, then only Mary, the spiritual action, will occupy the dwelling of your soul.[21]

Similarly in *On Jesus at the Age of Twelve* Aelred says that as the boy Jesus had to leave behind the spiritual delights of Jerusalem to return to Nazareth with the elders, so too must contemplatives 'put the needs of those in their care before the delights of contemplation'.[22]

Gilbert of Hoyland, the abbot of Swineshead who continued Bernard's sermon-commentary on the Song of Songs, argues that not only is labor in the world unavoidable in and in fact essential to the life of the *sponsa Christi*, but it is through that labor that she may fully come to contemplation. In Sermon 39 on the Song of Songs he writes:

The active life looks more toward [the bride's garden]; contemplation alone looks to [the bridegroom's]. Although the bride rejoices in hers, laboring with it and in her sweat feeding on its fruit, when she is led into his garden, nothing remains but delight alone. She guards her own garden but gazes upon his. Nor is she led into his garden except from her own, that is, from activity to the practice of contemplation.[23]

The life of Wulfric continues the tradition of John's cistercian literary forebears in showing concern for the way in which one

---

21. S. XIX in Assumptione sanctae Mariae, 18–21; CCCM IIA:151.
22. Jesu 3.31; CCCM 1:278 (ET CF 2:39).
23. SC 39.5; PL 184:210 (ET *Sermons on the Song of Songs* III, CF 26:482) (SC 40 in PL and ET; 39 in my forthcoming CCCM edition of Gilbert's works).

vowed to contemplative life may persevere in the search for the vision of God while faithfully responding to the needs of the world. The *Vita* insists that Wulfric was called by God to his cell and that throughout his life he was both wholly engaged in loving God as a *sponsa Christi* and wholly engaged in service to neighbor. John notes Wulfric's own awareness of the two portions of his life, his consciousness that in his service to those who come to him in need he seems a parish priest rather than an anchorite. But Wulfric's comments show a wry humor, a self-conscious recognition that his private prayer and public ministry complement one another, that he obtains in his nightly vigils just what he must supply in daily work. So John, by insisting that Wulfric in his lifetime successfully combined the lives of action and contemplation, extends the cistercian tradition by insisting on the necessity of such integration within contemplative life.

Although Wulfric had been neither monk nor cistercian, many of John's sources are both, a fact suggesting the reverence in which the anchorite was already held within the cistercian world and the importance of the anchorite's life for that community. As Wulfric had died in 1154, John was entirely dependent for information on his life and holiness from those who had known him, among them Walter, monk of Glastonbury; William, monk of Forde; and Henry, abbot of Tintern and Waverley.[24]

The *Vita* was apparently begun in about 1175 and completed in 1184, the year of the death of Bartholomew, bishop of Exeter, and of the consecration of Baldwin of Forde as Archbishop of Canterbury, as both of them appear as addressees in prefatory letters. The work survives in four manuscripts, three of which date from about 1200 and the fourth from shortly thereafter, all before John's death in 1214. Maurice Bell, editor of the *Vita*, says of the surviving manuscript witnesses that 'The great number of variations proves a considerable number of copies within a short period, and this attests the popularity of the work.'[25] The general appeal of

24. Cf. the discussion of John's sources by Pauline Matarasso, above, pp. 47, 49–52.
25. Wulf, p. lxxxi.

the text for both Cistercians and others concerned with solitary life appears in the fact that one of those four manuscripts (Camb. ms Univ. Lib. Add. 3037) also contains Reginald of Durham's life of the twelfth-century hermit Godric (written, Reginald says, 'not so much at the request as at the compulsion of Aelred of Rievaulx . . .'). A second (Brit. Lib. ms Cotton Faust. B.IV) had links to three cistercian houses, having been, according to Bell, copied by a scribe at Woburn and later owned by Holm Cultram, and containing two folios from Byland.[26]

The *Vita* begins with the two prefatory letters, one to Bartholomew, bishop of Exeter, and a second to Baldwin, archbishop of Canterbury. The work that follows contains three books of one hundred and five chapters, unevenly divided: Book One contains thirty chapters; Book Two twenty-eight; and Book Three forty-seven. In the letters John states his understanding of the significance of Wulfric's life for the history of the english church; in the body he makes that significance clear, establishing the divine call to Wulfric as a new christian coinage and showing his profound holiness and unremitting service to those in need. He portrays Wulfric as a man whose reputation grows as he does, who develops over the course of the work from initiation to perfection and so exercises an ever-widening influence, but who throughout his life of active involvement with the world remains within his cell in prayer and meditation, deriving the wisdom and grace he offers to his visitors from his nightly communion with the source of all wisdom. He emerges then as the characteristic cistercian bride of Christ, whose life combines and offers forth both the wine of contemplation and the milk of charity.

In the prefatory letters John states his purpose in writing the life and alerts the reader to his vision of Wulfric as one whose holiness comprises both the active and the contemplative lives and so as an *exemplum*, a model for contemplative life. To Bartholomew he writes:

> Indeed this man is meritorious in this world in his work of virtues, in the kindness of his oversight, in the word of

---

26. Wulf, pp. lxxvii-lxxx; and see also N. R. Ker, *Medieval Libraries of Great Britain* (2nd ed., London, Royal Historical Society, 1964) 23.

salvation, in revelation of the mysteries of God, and, especially, the most excellent of these, in his example of sanctity. In all these the world is in debt to him until this day.[27]

In the second prefatory letter, to Baldwin, John links Wulfric with such recent figures of english sanctity as Thomas of Canterbury, William of York,[28] and Godric of Finchale and anticipates later references to his building and ascending a mountain of contemplation, tacitly linking him to such traditional models of holiness through contemplation and service as Moses, Jesus, and Antony:

> We have that in which we may rejoice not only with our fathers because, behold, we also have a shoot of God in magnificence and glory, a fruit of heavenly earth. Now I say as in that day the mountains shall distill their sweetness. Would that there were also valleys that might receive that sweetness.[29]

This theme will recur through biblical reference and allusion in the course of the work that follows.

The *Vita* itself embodies in its tripartite structure Wulfric's movement from the world into the new life of holiness and so to new service, from the active life of the parish priest to the contemplative life of the anchorite, and then to the integration of those two lives within the anchorhold. Further, the structure shows Wulfric's passing through the stages of purgation, illumination, and judgment, as bride of Christ and saintly man of God.

THE *VITA*

The first book of the *Vita* establishes Wulfric as a beginner in anchoritic life, arguing that he is in the first place called to it by

27. Prologue, p. 7.
28. The reference to William might have startled Saint Bernard, one of his fiercest critics.
29. Wulf, pp. 11–12.

a messenger from God, then shows his growth in ascetic holiness. This is the stage of purgation and preparation, within which Wulfric takes the first steps of piety and virtue toward the later contemplative vision and increasing wisdom that will allow him to manifest God's judgment. It begins, after introducing Wulfric as a son of middle-class english folk (*mediocri Anglorum gente*) and as a parish priest who loves to hunt, with his call to anchoritic life. There is nothing particularly remarkable about the young Wulfric, nothing apparently to set him apart, to call God's attention to him. John gives no indication that before conversion the young man had spent any thought on the needs of those about him; he neither tells a tale of childhood virtue and special grace nor relates a story of childhood wickedness and consequent conversion. Wulfric is an ordinary man, an ordinary priest.

But one day a miracle happens, the first signal to the reader and to Wulfric himself that he has been set apart, not just to be changed, but to be made new. A stranger asks the young priest whether he has any of the king's new currency. At Wulfric's negative response, the man directs, 'Look in your pocket, and you will find tuppence ha'penny'. And he does. So, John says, 'God made a beginning of grace to his beloved Wulfric, bringing him the blessing of his sweetness, seeing him as another Nathaniel under the fig tree' (Jn 1:50). Further, John adds, the stranger is 'not undeservedly believed to be an angel of God, signifying a new man and demanding of him, as it were, new coinage'. John thus shows Wulfric to have been made new by grace, God's new currency. Further, for confirmation of this interpretation, he quotes Wulfric's own statement of the divine origins of his caller: 'He seemed to be a man, but he was no man'.[30]

This divine messenger, having revealed the meaning of his visit, next announces its purpose, Wulfric's *conversio morum*. He directs Wulfric into 'another place . . . from which you will persevere until the end of your life, afterwards to be called into the company of the saints'.[31] The *Vita* begins, then, by defining Wulfric's holiness

30. Ch. 1:13–14.
31. Ch. 1:14.

as an act of God and his life as one to which he was divinely ordained. Thus both Wulfric and those who read of him are able by understanding the origin of his vocation to recognize its meaning.

After the story of the miraculous call, much of the first book of the *Vita* is devoted to the formation of Wulfric and to his apprenticeship on the way to perfection in spiritual life. He quickly establishes himself as an ascetic, a man of unceasing prayer, and, finally, a miracle worker. He grows in virtue—in silence, speech, and humility—and he exercises himself in spiritual acts. Four chapters tell of the grace of the interior man (Ch. 2), of his vigils and *lectio divina* (Ch. 4), of his mind's *excessus* in prayer (Ch. 18), of his heart's stability in saying psalms (Ch. 19). As proof of his growth in the life of prayer and silence and of the reward for which the contemplative may hope. Two chapters tell of 'celestial visitation[s]'. Sometimes such visions explicitly declare his role as a holy man and a follower of Christ. So in one vision in this book Jesus and the twelve disciples appear to him as he stands within his cell, holding a cruet of oil, and Peter speaks to him, saying: 'Behold, the Lord is here; rise, hasten and come after us'. When Wulfric rises to follow the company, he spills the oil on his clothing and on the floor of his cell. Later, having confided his vision to a friend, he hears its interpretation: 'God has arranged to glorify this place by the work of your hands for the grace of healing and the work of virtues, and this is the oil poured out by your hand in this place and on your garment'.[32]

Other chapters recall the natural temptations and dangers that accompany the early stage of the contemplative life. So this book contains chapters on demonic temptation and a carnal lapse during sleep—not of explicit demonic cause—that Wulfric confesses publicly in the church.[33] In this book, then, the holy man is formed.

Even as Wulfric is finding his way in spiritual life, learning how to pray and keep silence, how to resist carnal and spiritual temptation, and beginning to receive glimpses of the spiritual delights he will later know, he is also beginning to serve those in need. As the first

32. Chs. 20:37–39; 11:24–26.
33. Ch. 12:26–27; 23:42–43.

book shows his growth in virtue and contemplative life, it also enunciates the reality of the world's interruption of that contemplative life, of the fact that the person called by God must always be ready to turn from the contemplative to the active life. So, for example, he accomplishes miraculous cures, exorcising a demon and healing two mutes, so successfully that one of them was able to speak not only English but French, with the result that Brihtric, priest of the parish of Haselbury, blamed the anchorite for having done more for a stranger than for his friend.[34]

In fact, it is through the close friendship between this priest and Wulfric that John is able to clarify the difference between the popular understanding, then as now, of the anchoritic life and the reality of that life. Wulfric, anxious about the barriers posed by his life of active service to his fulfillment of his vocation as an anchorite, enunciates the conflict between the view of the anchoritic life as one characterized by prayer and silence and the daily truth of that life, and reveals his own growing understanding of that truth. John writes of Brihtric:

> He was a man whose simplicity and humility were very like those of Blessed Wulfric, for he busied himself in the same way with psalms and prayers by day and night and, so far as his ministry allowed, gave himself up to perpetual watchings in his church. . . . Brihtric assisted [Wulfric] as if he were his Lord, humbly calling him *Dominum*, while Wulfric everywhere humbled himself in comparison with him, saying that Brihtric was really the anchorite of that place and he himself, who was always available for conferences, was more truly to be called parish priest.[35]

As Wulfric discovers for himself that the life of the anchorite is not, as he had thought, an opportunity for undistracted attention to God, to prayer, psalms, and vigils—that opportunity he could have had

34. Chs. 14–15:28–30; 17:31–34.
35. Chs. 16:30–31.

as a priest—he and the reader with him come to understand that the true anchorite, the holy man or woman called to solitary life, is someone who through very holiness, through life alone with God, unstintingly serves God's people.

In this passage as well John calls careful attention to Wulfric's real combination of virtue and prayer, defining Brihtric's life on the model of Wulfric's. So while Wulfric himself articulates his own consciousness of the daily reality of distraction from prayer, John anticipates that consciousness with a reminder that the substance of his life, the model he provides to those about him, is simplicity, humility, the saying of psalms and prayers, perpetual watchings. Indeed, John insists on the self-conscious similarity between Brihtric and Wulfric and anticipates later discussion of Wulfric's contemplative search when he says: 'there was a continuous friendly rivalry in mutual subjection and humility between these two young doves'.[36]

The first book of the *Vita*, then establishes the anchorite as someone holy in the ability to combine the lives of action and contemplation, loving God and serving neighbor. In it Wulfric is called, established, tested, and formed.

With the narrative of formation accomplished, Book Two shows the developing life of contemplation as Wulfric increasingly seeks the sight of God and delights in the search. This book shows his increasing sanctity, his greater powers of bringing the miraculous to pass; it marks the traditional stage of illumination.

Indeed, in this book Wulfric is surrounded by light, always in the works of John of Forde—as Hilary Costello has pointed out— a symbol of Divine Wisdom, of Christ, of understanding; for John contemplation is:

A type of vision . . . a vision of the face of Christ, of the eternal light that is in heaven, of the glory of the Lord. . . . In all this, contemplation is depicted as a place of light rather than darkness. From this point of view John of Ford must be placed unequivocally in the 'School of Light.'[37]

36. Ch. 16:31.
37. Hilary Costello, 'John of Ford and the Quest for Wisdom', *Cîteaux* 23 (1972) 152.

John emphasizes in Book Two that while all others sleep in the darkness of night, Wulfric watches: 'at dusk sending the crowds away and renewing his wings in his dawn, like a dove he flew to his window and rested there.' This dusk is indeed dawn for him, for at his window he finds 'the brilliance of the true light . . . his light, his joy'.[38]

While by night Wulfric seeks the light of God, he receives occasional anticipatory glimpses of that light in his cell and his eucharistic celebration. Candles burn and are not consumed, celestial light appears in the air. Extinguished light rekindles after he prays all night, not noticing the darkness, illuminated by celestial light and singing in the words of Psalm 26: *Dominus illuminatio mea et salus mea; quem timebo?*[39] So he grows as a contemplative, his understanding and closeness to Christ, the Wisdom of the Father, made visible.

As in the first chapter of Book One John defines Wulfric as a new coinage of God, in the first chapter of Book Two he defines Wulfric as a mature contemplative, a *sponsa Christi*. He not only notes Wulfric's experience of the brilliance of God but again implicitly reminds the reader of the anchorite's similarity to Moses, Jesus, and Antony when he 'at dusk . . . sent the crowds away and climbed his mountain to pray alone' . At the end of this introductory chapter he explicitly, in the words of the Song of Songs, links Wulfric with the bride, asking: 'Could it not be said of the blessed Wulfric, . . . of that man's soul, holy in the joy of his love, "This is my beloved; I am his"?' [Sg 1:16][40]

Again, as in the first chapter of Book One, here at the beginning of Book Two John enunciates the spiritual meaning of Wulfric's mature life as an anchorite within a discussion of the concrete details of that life, the constant demands of those about him on his time, attention, and wisdom. So the anchorite appears not only as the bride, the true lover of Christ, but as the dove of the Song of Songs, in his nightly vigils flying from the world to God and from God again to the world. The images of this chapter insist that Wulfric and by implication all

38. Ch. 31:48.
39. Ch. 32:49.
40. Ch. 31:48.

who would be like him must regularly mount from human need to the interior mountain for prayer and longing for the vision of God's face, but that at the same time, in the same way, they must seek out wisdom to take back to those who wait below. For even while busy with his own salvation, John says, Wulfric 'was concerned for others. He happily drew water from the fount of salvation which he would pour back upon those who had come to see him in the morning, people who could not draw the water themselves because the pool was deep'. John insists on the dual nature of Wulfric's role, emphasizing that to seek God the anchorite must 'dismiss the crowds', that he prays 'resting from the affairs of humankind . . . all the while celebrating Christ, apart so to speak from the cares of the world because all slept and dreamed'.[41]

Having begun by showing the source of Wulfric's holiness and wisdom, this book continues with a variety of miracles taking place within his oratory or the church into which his cell opens, miracles not only filled with the reception of divine light but insistently eucharistic. Water is turned to wine, bread miraculously multiplies, water which Wulfric forgets to bless becomes 'the pure water of penitence of the heart in the chalice of the Lord'.[42]

Wulfric also accomplishes miraculous cures in this book, in one case healing the virgin Emma while she, and apparently he, sleeps. In the narrative of this cure Emma wakes from a dream of Wulfric and says to her mother:

> Have no more fear for me in this illness, because by the grace of God and the man of God from Haselbury, behold I am healed. For he appeared to me in sleep; I came to him and was received by him, and when he offered me water that he had blessed in an overflowing cup, I tasted, and health and peace came to my interior parts.[43]

41. Ch. 31:48; cf. Is 12:3, Jn 4:11.
42. Ch. 49:66-68.
43. Ch. 42:58–59.

Then she describes the man, as John reports, saying, 'such and such is the man; such and such is the place'. John comments finally that: 'It was not enough that the blessed Wulfric healed when present or awake, but he did not fail to extend the generosity of his hand even when absent or asleep'.[44]

The miracles in this book—of light, of bread and wine, and of healing—reiterate Wulfric's similarity to Jesus. As the anchorite is like Jesus in dismissing the people so that he may ascend his mountain in prayer, so he is a worker of miracles, a conveyer of divine wisdom and power, one in whose presence water turns to wine, bread multiplies, and the sick are made whole.

It is also in this book that John begins to develop Wulfric's special relationship with cistercian monasticism, insisting especially on his attachment to the abbey of Forde. So, writing of his generosity and hospitality, John says that Wulfric 'freely overflowed in the riches of his simplicity upon the poor men of Forde, embracing them especially in the love of God and venerating them as angels of God'.[45] This special relationship was not without its costs, however; John reports that monks of Forde felt themselves obligated to visit him whenever passing.[46] But the heart of Wulfric, says John, 'or rather of Jesus Christ himself, tightly clasped all who professed *Cisterciensis religionis*, lifting up their life with highest praises, directing all who came to him to a similar conversion of life and sending them without hesitation [*sine cunctatione*] to that order'. Indeed he 'said them to be angels of God in their rejection of food and clothing, in discipline, in love, and finally in all holiness'.[47]

A specific instance in this book of Wulfric's attachment to the Cistercian Order and of his counseling men to become monks there appears in the conversion of Henry, later abbot of Tintern and Waverley. It was Henry himself who many years later told John of Wulfric's role in his conversion, referring to it as evidence of the anchorite's holiness and prophetic power. After active participation

44. Ch. 42:59
45. Ch. 47:65.
46. Ch. 72:99.
47. Ch. 48:66.

in a band of those brigands who tormented medieval Europe, Henry recalls, he came to Haselbury in a beginning of repentance to ask the blessing of Wulfric, whom he had never met. Arriving during Mass, he heard Wulfric pray for a friend; immediately thereafter Wulfric came to meet him, greeting him with the words: 'Today I have said a collect for you at Mass'. Then as both men wept, Wulfric added, 'How happy would the man be to whom it was given to do what you are about to do'. To Henry's protests of unworthiness, Wulfric responded, in terms recalling the call of Francis of Assisi: 'To that church that you have violently plundered, you are to make recompense'. After a time of turning again from God, John concludes, Henry became a novice at Tintern, then was 'called into the ministry of abbot'.[48]

Wulfric's relationship with the Cistercians further appears in a story linking Wulfric, Henry, and Bernard of Clairvaux. Bernard, anxious about the implications of his efforts to resolve the papal schism, once asked Abbot Henry to request prayer for him from Wulfric. Henry, coming to Wulfric, began his request, by explaining: 'Blessed Bernard sends me to you that you may pray the Lord for a certain sin on account of which he greatly fears for his soul'. Wulfric, however, sharply interrupted, asking, 'Why did he wish on his own to usurp the knowledge of God's secrets?' Then he added, 'Truly God receives his penitence and does not impute this thing to him as sin'.[49]

John uses both of these narratives, the conversion of Henry and the communication with Bernard, not only to show Wulfric's close relationship with cistercian monasticism but by means of them to establish Wulfric's growing powers as a prophet. It is Wulfric who forsees Henry's monastic vocation and tells him of it, who prays for him before he arrives, and who recognizes him on first meeting as the one for whom the prayer was spoken. In fact, John titles the chapter that contains this narrative 'Of the Conversion of Abbot Henry of Waverley by Him [Wulfric] Prophesied'.[50] Henry's own account

48. Ch. 50:68–71.
49. Ch. 54:78–79.
50. Ch. 50:68.

of the experience insists on Wulfric's prophetic powers, which he experiences again years after the initial meeting, saying to Wulfric: 'I, Lord, am that man to whom you formerly declared those things that now by the grace of God have been accomplished in me; and behold before your face are the fruits of your prophecy'.[51] Again, Wulfric knows of Bernard's sin of presumption in attempting to intercede in the schism—not, one would think, a grave wrongdoing—from a distance and anticipates the request for forgiveness and communicates God's judgment, so bringing back to the world the wisdom he has previously received.

The absence of cistercian opportunities for women in the twelfth century appears in Wulfric's calling the woman Matilda not to cenobitic life, as he presumably would have done had she been a man, but to life as an anchoress. In this narrative John again shows the anchorite's power not only to counsel and convert but also to speak for God. This call begins when he sends for the woman, whom he has apparently never met, then announces to her in terms much like those spoken in his own call by the angelic visitor: 'In anchoritic life [*professione*] you will serve God for fifteen years in Wareham, and, at last, the sixteenth year will be the end of your life. Then you will proceed to your Lord with joy, because, behold, your mansion in heaven is prepared for you'.[52] So Matilda becomes an anchoress, called by Wulfric, with both her earthly life and heavenly reward set forth by him.

The third book contains the miracles, judgments, and prophecies of the mature man of God. Now Wulfric has been recognized by the world in Haselbury and beyond: he prophesies the death of Henry I and the reign of Stephen,[53] he chastises, curses, and again heals. Having established himself as a holy man full of God's wisdom, constantly in touch with God's guidance and grace, he is also seasoned as one in service to those in need. In this stage of the life he is finally indeed the 'hinge-man' of whom Peter Brown writes, one

51. Ch. 50:72.
52. Ch. 56:82.
53. Chs. 90–91:116–118.

of those whom Christopher Holdsworth describes as liminal, living 'on a frontier' and there exercising spiritual power 'through counsel, curing, healing, and prophecy'.[54] While he has been seen to exercise that power, in those ways, throughout the *Vita*, it is in Book Three that he comes into his own as the man of God. By the end of the book, in fact, he has progressed beyond purgation and illumination to become no longer merely a new man of God, a *sponsa Christi*, but a man of power and authority and a saint. So John ends the work not with his death, but with revelations and miracles wrought by him after death.

Book Three begins, as did Books One and Two, with a narrative defining the life stage and current role and power of the anchorite. In this first chapter as in the earlier ones Wulfric speaks as a man of holiness, insight, and prophecy, but now also as one able to pronounce God's judgment and to grant or, as in the first episode of the book, to withhold mercy. The chapter begins abruptly, with a rich and upright woman come to consult with Wulfric about the health of her soul. Suddenly Wulfric calls out for his servant and sends him to forbid a certain man, in the name of God, from crossing the bridge outside the city to come to him, 'because I am going to do nothing for him'. Upon hearing of the ban, the man 'begins to wail vehemently, falling on the earth and weeping as though in childbirth'. At this the servant, and then the woman caller, plead for Wulfric's forgiveness of the man, but the anchorite refuses all mercy, saying 'I do not spare, and I will not have mercy', and again 'I do not wish to and I am not able to have mercy'.[55]

In this passage Wulfric is no longer merely a seeker for illumination and wisdom but one who has received that wisdom and become fully able to exercise it. He is again as in the previous books portrayed as Christlike, though now not as someone who leaves behind the people to ascend the mountain of prayer, but as judge, voicer of God's judgment. So at the end of this episode John makes the association explicit, writing that the incident is to be considered

54. Holdsworth, pp. 57, 59.
55. Wulf, Ch. 59:88–89.

with fear in recognition of the 'wrath of God that closed to this wretch the way to the man [Wulfric] and seized up the bridge of mercy':

> And at the last day he will certainly not be able to cross the bridge; then in fact he will hear the sentence full of indignation, the bitter and unbearable word: 'Depart from me, for I do not know you.' And then, as he weeps and wails, from the throne of justice will come the inexorable reply: 'What I have written, I have written.'[56]

So John defines Wulfric now as having moved into a final stage of holiness, now become a spokesman for God, someone who anticipates God's judgment. Although Bell comments that 'this is a queer tale',[57] both its details and its implications presenting a Wulfric who seems arbitrary and unsympathetic, its purpose is clear: he is a man who has God's authority to loose and unloose, to forgive or to damn.

In this book Wulfric repeatedly cures, prophesies conception and death, curses and denounces, and even chastises Matilda, King Stephen's queen, for refusing recognition to a noblewoman come to call on her. The book is full, in fact, of what John refers to as 'the innumerable signs of the man of God'.[58]

The book concludes with the final proof of Wulfric's sanctity, his power beyond the grave. After his death, whose date he has predicted, an altercation over possession of his body breaks out. The bishop buries him in his cell, associating him thereafter with Saint Paul,[59] and Osbern, now the priest of Haselbury, twice moves and reburies his body out of fear for its safety. First moving the body to a place on the north side of the altar, Osbern later moves it again, now 'hiding his secret between God and himself in the western part of the church'.[60]

---

56. Ch. 59:89–90.
57. P. liii..
58. Wulf, Ch. 97:122.
59. Ch. 101:127–129.
60. Ch. 102:130.

John follows these events, emphasizing the significance of the death of Wulfric and the public awareness of his sanctity, with three chapters telling of the revelations and cures wrought by him. In the first of these, noted in the chapter title as 'believed to be angelic',[61] a man dressed as a pilgrim appears to Osbern requesting a memorial of 'Wulfric, blessed and beloved by God'. When Osbern replies that nothing remains other than those things consecrated for sacred use, which he has no right to give away, the pilgrim directs him to a chest containing a bowl and spoon 'with which he used to eat', both apparently unknown to Osbern. Having given these to the pilgrim and closed the chest, Osbern turns to discover him vanished. Searching everywhere and finding no trace of him, Osbern becomes persuaded that this visitor was 'a more than earthly man'. So John concludes that this visitation was intended 'to lead the sons of men to the embrace of the blessed Wulfric'.[62] And as Wulfric's initial call to holy life had long before been accomplished by a stranger who 'seemed to be a man, but . . . was no man',[63] so the first revelation of Wulfric's power after his death is similarly proclaimed.

In the final chapter of the *Vita,* the woman Leviva receives a vision telling her to heal her husband's stomach problems by giving him a drink of dust from Wulfric's tomb dissolved in water. After repeatedly delaying out of fear before the tomb, she finally does as she has been told, with the effect that her husband—'half alive, or rather nearly dead'—rises up 'as from the dead'. When others, hearing of the miraculous cure, come to her, she heals many with the remains of the potion. John concludes: 'And so the whole church of God knows that the blessed Wulfric is in the glory of God the Father, and is at hand if someone shall require him; indeed let him say as before it was said, "Behold, I am ready" '.[64] So as Wulfric throughout his life combined love of God with love and service of neighbor, even in death, in the eternal presence of God, he continues to bend to the need of those who wait.

---

61. Ch. 103:130.
62. Ch. 103:130–131.
63. Ch. 1:14.
64. Ch. 105:134; cf. Gen 46:2, Is 52:6.58:9.

John reveals his understanding of Wulfric as one who integrated the active and contemplative lives not only through the arrangement of the *Vita* and the narratives that shape it, but through his use of the Song of Songs to define the holy man, sometimes in language and imagery very close to what he will later, in his Sermons on the Song of Songs, use for the bride of Wisdom, the true contemplative. For Wulfric is for John indeed the Bride, the beloved of Christ.

It is in Chapter 31, discussed above,[65] that John most clearly enunciates this understanding of Wulfric. In this chapter, titled 'Of Wulfric's Lauds', he writes of Wulfric as 'one of the guards who patrols the city by night, keeping watch while Jerusalem sleeps in the night of her infirmity and dispensing the grace received during that night from God'. This passage, noting Wulfric's vision of 'the brilliance of the true light . . . his light, his joy', shows him as 'like a dove flying to his window and resting there', there finding his joy in the brilliance of the true light and 'busying himself with his own salvation'.[66]

Even during this time of truest solitude with God, his gazing like a dove on the light of God, John insists, however, Wulfric does not leave behind his concern for the world and his service of ministry, for he combines the contemplative joys of vision and celebration with service to others, busying himself with his own salvation while drawing water of salvation for those who can not draw it themselves, gathering 'the wealth of salvation' that 'came to him from every direction as if to a beacon raised on high' and then 'passing freely and ungrudgingly to others the grace he had received'.[67]

Many years later John returns to the theme of the vigils of the contemplative, reiterating the way in which that contemplative looks on God and then dispenses to the community the grace he found there. In Sermon 16 on the Song of Songs he writes of those who looked on Jesus in the flesh:

65. See pp. 81–82 above.
66. Ch. 31:48.
67. Ch. 31:48.

Burning like the sun with a twofold flame of charity, [they] suffered violent constraint as to which love they should more especially abandon themselves to. For to be dissolved and to be with Christ was their supreme desire, but the other charity, though less in its affective power but more irresistible in its strength, compelled them to think of their little ones and to bide with them until they were weaned. Their love for God was sweeter, but the love for his sons was more pressing. The one was more peaceful, the other more insistent. And indeed this love towards one's neighbor is of a lesser kind, but in the dispensation of the wisdom of God, disposing all within his house wisely and sweetly, there was a tranquil readiness for the greater to yield and become the servant of the less. . . . [68]

Again in this sermon as in the *Vita*'s narrative of the friendship and rivalry in virtue and piety between Wulfric and Brihtric, John associates those who combine service to neighbor with love of God with doves, returning to the image of the wisdom brought from God to humans in need as water sought by those doves:

Doves . . . are artless in their innocence, swift in flight, united in love, fruitful in offspring, tender in sighing. So too, they [the first followers of Jesus] were innocent in bearing injuries without retaliation, swift in bestowing a kindness, eager in reviving and preserving charity, zealous in bringing to life the little buds of an ever-growing piety devoted to maturing and forming them. . . . How bewildering, how wonderful, these words from so many ages before, greeting from afar those men of virtue, who are those 'who fly like a cloud and like doves to their windows!'

This double flight, what is its purpose in these great friends of God? They fly for our sake, they fly back for their own sake. They fly like clouds to make us fruitful, they

68. SC 16.4; CCCM 17:143 (CF 39:19–20).

fly back to their windows to ponder themselves. Externally they are usefully at work; internally they are humbly at rest. . . . As they freely received the rain coming down to them from above, so they freely poured it back to us down below. For rain is certainly free, coming down from the pure and most loving will of him who is the father of rain; through the willing service of these men he sends it out to purify and make fruitful the will of men. . . . In this service they claim no credit for themselves but rather for God who gives the rain and the increase; they await only the eternal reward of their toil. And then they are doves at their windows, when in all simplicity they preach to us the word of life, not seeking our possessions but ourselves.[69]

These words, written some twenty years after the *Vita*, continue the argument of that early work of the prior of Forde, the argument that true contemplatives, true doves, are known by their works of contemplation and service. So John in his sermon defines the pastor and the teacher in precisely the same terms as twenty years before he had defined the anchorite, the holy man of God. In their preface to John's sermons on the Song of Songs, Edmund Mikkers and Hilary Costello note that the *Vita S. Wulfrici* 'abounds in texts from the Song of Songs, a fact proving that John had for a long time [before writing the sermons] been meditating on this work'.[70] Indeed John is already at work in that early examination of the one called by God to holy life to define him as the *sponsa Christi* and, through him, to define the *sponsa Christi* as the one who gazes on God's wisdom while dispensing its benefits to 'the little ones'.

CONCLUSION

In the course of the *Vita*, John shows Wulfric's call to anchoritic life and his development as a holy man. From beginning to end

69. SC 16:5–6; CCCM 17:143–144 (CF 39:21–22).
70. CCM 17:xiv.

Wulfric's life as an anchorite blends contemplation and service, the one informing the other. The young man is new-coined, a second Nathaniel, called by God to new life. Having entered upon that life he passes through nights of prayer and days of humble service, gazing upward to love and look upon God while reaching downward to those who come to him in hunger, pain, repentance, sorrow, or grief. He converts men and women from wrongdoing to become cenobites or anchorites; he speaks sharply to the strong and gently to the weak; he forgives and curses, prophesies, reveals, and blesses. So he models for John's audience the contemplative life as a life of holiness, called forth, shaped, and illuminated by God in the hours of active service as in the hours of silent prayer.

The older view of Wulfric as essentially a man of action and service is thus incomplete, in serious ways untrue to John's essential understanding of the anchorite of Haselbury and to John's purpose in writing the *Vita*. For John writes explicitly to show Wulfric as a model of modern—twelfth-century—english Christianity, someone who continues the tradition of holiness in the english church, in fact a contemplative, an imitator of Moses, Jesus, and Antony, one illuminated by God's wisdom. John depicts Wulfric as a man called by God away from the world, a man of simplicity and wisdom, a lover and imitator of Christ. Finally he shows Wulfric to be a contemplative, a *sponsa Christi*, who must make opportunities for contemplation when freed from obligation to the crowds to whose needs he is daily bound, needs he is able to supply precisely because of his nights of vision. John's life of Wulfric is above all a portrait of the reality of contemplative life and a model for the living of such a life.

In this portrait John insists that the contemplative, like all Christians, must be unceasing in service to the neighbor while urgent in the search for the sight of God. So he reconciles the roles of Leah and Rachel, of Martha and Mary, so he demonstrates the existence of such holy integration in his modern England, so he resolves the traditional cistercian ambivalence about the conflicting appeal and merits of the eremitic and the cenobitic life: so he provides an exemplum for cistercian contemplative theology.

Hilary Costello, OCSO

Secretarius Dominici Pectoris
Saint John's Gospel
in John of Forde

ALTHOUGH JOHN of Forde quotes spontaneously and extensively from all the books of the New Testament, he appears to have a predilection for the fourth gospel. Some statistics will help to establish this. While there are six columns of references to Saint John's Gospel in the Index, Saint Luke's Gospel, which is the longest, has only four columns of quotations. Saint Matthew's Gospel which is the next longest has five columns. So Saint John's Gospel is comparatively more quoted than the others.

The reason for this predilection may be found in certain themes that lie at the heart of his thought. For the purposes of this study I have selected just four of these themes:

1. *In sinu Patris*: 'In the bosom of the Father'.
2. *Tu fons caritatis*: 'You are the source of Love'.
3. The Word.
4. Jesus and the Father.

Other important themes, such as the glorification of Jesus, which hold an equally important place in John's thought, will—for lack of space—have to be left to another paper at some future date.

Before we start to consider these themes, we need to say a few words about John of Forde's notable admiration for the 'disciple whom Jesus loved', whom he calls '*secretarius dominici pectoris*',[1]

1. Sermon 26.5 (*John of Ford: Sermons on The Song of Songs*, translated by Wendy Mary Beckett, vol. 2:165).

which far from meaning 'the Lords' secretary', can be translated as 'the confidant of the secrets of Jesus' heart'.

Secretarius does not occur in classical Latin. *Secretarium* does. It comes from the verb *secernere*, to set apart. It could be a desert place or a hiding place. If you hide something within yourself it becomes a secret. If you divulge it to a very close friend, it is still something set apart; it is still a secret. That person becomes your confidant—a friend to whom you have revealed your 'secret', your most intimate thought. Later, it became a legal term for a court counsellor. But John is using it for the friend who rested on Jesus' breast and heard his most intimate secret revelations of love.

We refer to the fourth gospel as Saint John's Gospel. But John himself does not refer to himself by name. Remember that we are, as it were, in the twelfth century; we do not as yet ask the twentieth century question: 'Who wrote the fourth gospel?' and reject Saint John's authorship. No, it was written by Saint John, a man of great modesty:

> Like Saint Paul, who did not talk of his ecstasies, but with the greatest wisdom preserved the modest anonymity of the third person when he said, 'I know a man in Christ who was caught up into paradise and right into the third heaven', so too the disciple Jesus loved, when he wanted to refer to himself, used this lovely expression to identify himself, almost as if it were his own name. He then went on to speak of the way he reclined on Jesus' breast, an even more expressive indication of love.[2]

It is this disciple, Saint John, so beloved of Jesus, who heard the words that flowed superabundantly from Jesus' own lips: 'Only words like these are words of strength, only they are living and lifegiving. Only those who listen to them are alive, and whoever listens to them, although in the grave, rises immediately to life'.[3]

2. 45.2 (3:180).
3. 21.7 (2:99).

John of Forde contrasts the whole of the rigid message and law of the Old Testament with the gentle and loving law of Christ. But it was the beloved disciple who understood the full depth of this love. He is the one who tells us that 'grace and truth have come through Jesus Christ' [Jn 1:17].

IN SINU PATRIS

Grace and truth—these are rich examples of the twins we find in Scripture. The mysteries of Christ and the Church are too deep to be understood by the human mind. Yet God has given us keys that will open up the Scriptures for us. These keys come in pairs: wisdom and prudence; understanding and activity (*operatio*); love of God and love of neighbour. Justice and truth are said to be united in a kiss. But above all, it is grace and truth that have come into being through Jesus Christ.[4]

These two words, grace and truth, have a very deep and powerful meaning in John of Forde's theology. We must remember that John, like all his contemporaries, always sees Christ and the Church as a complete unity, an indivisible whole, united in the love of the Father. Jesus Christ has received from the Father the infinite fullness of love and the incomprehensible reality that is God. This love and this reality have been given to the Church, not because the Church is a separate entity united with Christ, but because it is a unity with Christ, a unity which is Head and Body. He would certainly maintain the unity of Christ and the Church in a way that implies all the riches belonging to the Head are communicated to the Body.

Christ received this superabundance of 'grace and truth' because he was from the beginning 'in the bosom of the Father'. In a subtle way John lifts our contemplation of this mystery of Christ and the Church to the ultimate vision of his glory. Our eyes too will have seen this vision, if we have become worthy to be named 'bride', *sponsa*. There can be no doubt that Saint John had this vision:

4. 72.8 (5:128).

Blessed indeed were those eyes that saw what they saw. They saw the Only-begotten in the bosom of the Father, they saw him whom the angels themselves long to look at. They were considered worthy, not once or twice or three times, but daily and almost continually to contemplate him, and by the constant sight of that lovely and compelling countenance, to seal that image of the living God within them which is the loving imprint of the light from God's own face.[5]

The phrase 'in the bosom of the Father' occurs at least twenty times in these sermons. Moreover, there are other equivalent phrases: 'in the heart of the Father' (*in corde Patris*),[6] 'in the soul of the Father' (*in anima Patris*),[7] and 'from the deep love of the Father' (*ex utero Patris*),[8] which is virtually the same but is an adaptation of Ps 109:3: 'from the womb before the daystar I begot thee'.

This interesting, if a little complex, phrase in John's thought sums up succinctly the relationship of Father to Son and Son to Father in the mystery of the Trinity. There is not much we can say about this relationship before time began, before the whole of creation was set in motion. John talks of it in connection with the 'generation of the Word' within the Trinity and this must always be totally beyond human comprehension. 'The secret mystery of the divine generation'[9] touches on a theme in western theology which is not exactly negative (apophatic) theology but is very close to it. In fact he warns us off making too many assertions about the mystery because we simply cannot begin to grasp it, and there is real danger of losing reverence for the Trinity by getting tangled up with useless questions.

At the same time we should not just remain silent. From the beginning before time, in the Eternity that is God, the Father generated

5. 16.2 (2:17).
6. 14.3 (1:253); 106.7 (7:71).
7. 14.3 (1:254); 39.5 (3:121).
8. 7.5 (1:155); 14.2 (1:252).
9. 7.1 *divinae generationis arcanum* (1:149).

his Son who is totally equal to himself. Thus they are one Light, one Heat, one Wisdom, one Truth, one Holiness. Pseudo-Dionysius himself would not have denied this, even though he rejects it in favour of a Not-truth that is Super-truth, and so forth.

John is more circumspect and decidedly more aesthetic. He says:

> We were wholly unable to come near you, the dawning splendour of light eternal, and yet you came near to us by that same free and innate goodness with which, born from the Father's womb before the daystar, you flashed out so wonderfully in the saints' first splendours.[10]

So then, a few lines further on he has this sentence, worthy of long meditation, which combines and harmonizes the positive and negative and is, if I may say so, on a higher plane:

> You were the great light hidden in the bosom of your Father; you came forth from your retreat into our market-place. You became a great light for the great, and a small lamp for little ones—a lamp not only visible to our eyes but palpable to our touch.[11]

This brings us to the second point: the choice of Mary to be the Mother of Jesus. We are invited to imagine God looking out from this hidden place at the world he has created, and making a decision. He is going to choose someone:

> When he was still in his most holy and hidden resting place, the bosom of the Father, he looked on the lowliness of the handmaid whom they call blessed. For she found grace most richly in his eyes, and not for herself only, but for all generations that are to come.[12]

10. 7.5 (1:155).
11. 7.5 (1:156).
12. 19.2 (2:62).

So Mary was chosen. John implies that she was chosen from eternity. But he brings in two other observations here. She was given the unique and incommunicable privilege of being called his mother, so that he was the Son of the Most High *and* the son of the most lowly. Then, following on from that, there is an unchangeable law (a reference perhaps to Daniel 6:15 where the law of the Medes and Persians cannot be changed) that everyone who humbles himself will be exalted. Humility, as a vital element in the quality of life for all Christians, is Mary's especial endowment and bequest to humankind.[13]

The third point is that the Word came from the bosom of the Father precisely in order to create the Church. The word *Sponsa* in John's commentary has as its primary meaning the Church, unless John says explicitly that he is referring to the soul. For example, in Sermon 33, which is entirely devoted to the Church, John insists that the house built by Jesus for his Bride, the Church, was firmly constructed on solid foundations. It was for this reason that the true Solomon came down from heaven: to give his whole heart to the task of building this house, the Church. He would remain here until it was completed. He would not go back to his bed of repose, the bosom of the Father, until he had found a place for the Lord. He carved out from his own self and in his own self the columns of the Church, his Bride.[14]

Fourthly, coming down to the level of the individual, i.e. any soul that loves God,[15] John, like Guerric of Igny, compares the spiritual life to a garden, but without the trivial sentimentality of later writers. Here we find hedges, pruning, spade-work, dung on well-manured ground and so forth. This garden is rich with blossoming flowers, aromatic enough to draw Jesus by its very fragrance from the Father's bosom, provided we are not apathetic.[16]

13. *Ibid.*
14. 33.8 (3:59–60).
15. 44.6 (3:172).
16. 44.4–6 (3:169–173). Cf. Guerric of Igny, 'A Sermon for Arousing Devotion at Psalmody,' *Liturgical Sermons*, Vol. 2; Cistercian Fathers Series 32 (1971) 213–218.

On this same level, John describes his own personal experience. With considerable restraint he tells us that the Lord has visited him and favoured him with an unimaginable revelation of the Father's love in a gentle whisper. John allows himself a certain indulgence here when he says, 'I see and understand that he has stolen quietly from his Father's bosom to tell us truly of his Father and explain what is within his bosom.'[17] It is on this same level of meaning that he addresses those few who have merited a greater intimacy with the Word and have been given the name *sponsa*, bride,[18] though not in the same manner as the Church.

Although John himself received some visitation, some vision of God, he did not in any way confuse this with the final vision which is reserved for the next life. For him, as for Saint Bernard and Guerric, this ultimate vision is the 'naked truth', *nuda veritas*, given to the Church in her triumphant circle of saints when all the shadows and images are removed and she sees God face to face. This is the *future* marriage, 'wedded to him at the end of time', when the Church as the body of all the saints will see quite openly 'the Only-Begotten in the Father's bosom'.[19]

We should add a fifth point here: this presence can be removed. During the Interdict which began in 1208, the sacraments were not allowed to the english people and it seemed that the Lord had gone away. 'You have fled from us.' John complains, 'You have withdrawn to your royal retreat, the bosom of your Father.'[20] Clearly this was considered a great tragedy for the whole country.

But it is also clear that not every going away is considered a tragedy. This is the sixth and final point concerning this phrase *in sinu Patris*. At the Ascension Christ went back to his place in heaven where he will remain in glory in his Father's bosom[21] and therefore complete the great circle of our salvation. John recommends that we

17. 43.9 (3:162).
18. 29.2 (3:2–3).
19. 72.6 (5:125).
20. 41.8 (3:143).
21. 80.7 (5:227–228).

should ponder this final stage deeply in the hope that some spark of this glory may come to each of us.

The Church

The Church, which is Christ's bride, speaks with a certain audacity of the Word of God. She does not hesitate to call him 'my Beloved' and even recalls the superabundant love he has shown her and the ineffable words he has revealed to her, words that cannot be spoken.[23] The reason for this is that Jesus' words must be understood on several levels of meaning.[24] He speaks human words, yes. We can understand them on the human level. But they should not be understood *only* on that level. They are also the words of the Father's Only-begotten Son who utters the hidden mysteries of God with his divine lips.[25] John of Forde has a memorable phrase to describe what cannot be described: *Ineffabilia prorsus et modo loquitur ineffabili*,[26] which Sister Wendy Mary Beckett has translated, 'He speaks of completely ineffable things, and in an ineffable manner'. There is a challenge here. Who can understand these things? Who is worthy? Who could penetrate the words that Jesus has heard from the Father? (Perhaps preachers and teachers of the Gospels who are a bit too ready to tell us exactly what Jesus meant could take John of Forde's advice to heart).

Who can listen to and understand these words? Each of us, no doubt. But that is not the first answer. 'Listen' says our John, 'listen, O Church of God. To you the words are spoken, and to you alone have been given ears that can hear'.[27]

22. 13.10: 'You are the source of Love' (1:247).
23. 4.1 (1:113).
24. 57.1 (4:138).
25. 21.7 (2:101).
26. 21.7 (2:101).
27. 13.6 (1:241).

John has his own 'hymn to love' coming near the beginning of his commentary in Sermon 13, just as Bernard, in Sermon 83 *super Cantica*, had his own special hymn to love towards the end of his commentary and indeed towards the end of his life. We should not try to compare them. Each has his own style. Bernard, the ultimate master of rhetoric, sweeps the reader up with him into an impetuous storm of incomparable praise of the Word, the Bridegroom of the soul. John, on the contrary, takes us with him on a more tranquil sea that flows from the very Being of God as the Father gazes at the Church in the light of his Only Son.

> Listen! Consider the great Majesty of him who has loved you, how he has loved you from all eternity, how undeserved this love has been, how great it is.[28]

In the beginning God created the world out of his power and his love. Much later the Father sent his Son to redeem the world. For thirty years Jesus kept himself to himself. Then at last he broke his silence, opened his mouth, and poured out the sweet honey of his lips.

> So the Wisdom of God has come, preaching to the world the love of God. And Jesus cries out: 'God so loved the world as to give his Only-Begotten Son'.[29]

The theme of love quite naturally dominates these sermons from the Prologue on. In Sermon 109 John begins with the distinction between three classical forms of love: the love with which God loves; the love by which he is loved; and that love by which we love our neighbour in God. This last love is a fire, a fire that cannot be extinguished. The primary source of this inextinguishable love is God's love for us. John insists on this:

---

28. 13.6 (1:241). The resounding paeon of praise occupies most of this sermon.
29. 13.5 (1:241).

God gave the world incontrovertible evidence which the world cannot hesitate to accept, that 'he so loved the world that he gave his Only Son'.[30]

John has an interesting sentence here: 'He gave this evidence in the waters, he gave it also in the floods'. It is clear, of course, that he is referring to the waters of suffering and death that Jesus passed through and sailed home safely to the harbour of his resurrection and eternal life with his Father. The background to this reference to water seems to be the israelitic passage through the Red Sea or through the Jordan to the Promised Land. And maybe there is also a hidden reference to Jonah being thrown into the waters of the hurricane and swallowed by the great sea-monster, for John quotes Ps 69:1 ('the waters have come into my soul'), and Lam 3:54 ('the waves overwhelmed me')—applying them to Christ's death.

The Individual

This same sermon (109) is concerned mainly with the love between God and the Church. John remains throughout it on the allegorical level. Many of the sermons, on the contrary, are on the personal level. This is true of Sermon 43, in which John gives some personal hints, couched in terms that could be applied to almost any individual searching for God, about his own experience of the love God has shown him. He is talking of the ways that the Lord has come to him personally. The ways are, I think, classical. You find them in Saint Bernard's Sermons 18 and 85 *super Cantica*, expressed differently, of course, but still recognizable.

The initial pain of self-analysis and the realization of sinfulness—the feeling of total unworthiness of the beginner—is followed by a period of psychological and spiritual release when the young person feels overwhelmed by a feeling of pardon—*spem veniae*—and God's love for him or her. After that there follows once more a period of darkness and confusion when the person feels bereft of God for ever.

---

30. 109.2 (7:104).

But perseverance in meditation on the Gospels and the life of Jesus, his birth, his passion and death, his humility and perhaps his miracles, leads once more to the experience of being loved again and called to much greater intimacy with the Lord: 'I feel sure he has called me to the wedding feast'. 'Everything then becomes a delight, everything is lit up and sparkles, all things become fragrant and perfumed for me, every single thing has its own special flavour'.[31]

As with all the mystics, however, John warns us that this experience is all too rare and too brief. To use the well-worn phrase, 'the night of the spirit' invades the soul. The Lord goes away, retires to his marriage chamber, his own place.

After these preliminary visitations, John goes on to describe a much more elevated type. This is expressed in mystical language. Whether it indicates that John himself was a mystic is another question. This is what he says: 'So sweet is the mystery that it cannot be explained, but in his overflowing grace he reveals it, as it were, in a gentle whisper'.[32] This experience is given by the Father from his love, the love by which 'he so loved the world that he sent his Only-begotten Son' [Jn 3:16].

We are warned and assured that this experience is given only to those souls that have been fully healed by the touch of Jesus and can listen to him as to a Master (Jn 3:2). Anointed by Jesus, the soul herself can now anoint Jesus—a reference to Nicodemus, who came with spices to anoint Jesus' body after his death (Jn 19:39). He was now able to follow Jesus in the daylight rather than come to him only by night as he had done earlier in Saint John's Gospel. Previously Nicodemus was a type of the sensual person, not yet ready to understand the things of God. He was no doubt a master in Israel, but a mere recruit in christian piety, says John, contrasting the jewish law with christian mysticism, and finding the former very much wanting. Nicodemus was not yet able to listen to the Master of humility, Jesus.[33] All this refers to Chapter 3 of the Fourth Gospel.

---

31. 43.5: *Ita cuncta placent, cuncta splendent, omnia redolent, singula sapiunt* (3:159).
32. 43.9 (3:161).
33. 43.10 (3:163–164).

When we next hear of Nicodemus in Chapter 19, he comes to anoint Jesus. He is now a type of the perfect christian soul who follows Jesus, the True Light, and is no longer in darkness.

Going on from this, yet still remaining with the Fourth Gospel, John of Forde raises our spirits to the heights in two ways. First of all, this personal visitation takes place when Jesus comes and makes his abode in us [Jn 14:23].[34] Secondly, this visitation is a foretaste of the heavenly dwelling when Jesus goes to prepare a place for us. He who dwells eternally in the bosom of the Father takes us back with him after our death to dwell with him in the Father.

THE THEME OF THE WORD

This leads us quite naturally to the theme of the Word. Theologically this part of my paper should have come much earlier, but I have placed it here because I want to look at it from a psycho-spiritual viewpoint. If we leave on one side the detailed references to the second half of the Song of Songs, the most frequently quoted text in John of Forde's Commentary is Jn 1:14: 'The Word was made flesh and dwelt among us'.

Praise of the Word

The Evangelist begins at the beginning, before the world came into being. He begins with the Word who was with the Father. John of Forde, on the contrary, begins where he is. A weak mortal man, a man of flesh, he can only look up with amazement at the condescension of the Word who comes down to him.

> I embrace the loving condescension, I marvel at the Wisdom, I give thanks for the tender mercy which 'lowered his heavens' [when] 'the Word was made flesh'.[35]

34. 43.11 (3:164).
35. 33.2 (3:51).

But this act of infinite humility makes it now possible for this man of flesh to climb up the ladder to meet the Word.

John's response to this loving-kindness is a song of praise to the Word. Praise worthy of the Word will elude all the efforts of someone still on this earth, but praise there must be. Only in the heavenly kingdom will it be possible to give full and worthy praise and glory to him. John of Forde breaks out into a great song of joy:

> In the highest heaven is his glory,
>   supremely radiant and shining.
> There love burns bright
>   and understanding is vigorous,
> There goodwill is ever eager
>   and memory wide awake.
> There no anxiety distracts,
>   no difficulty presses, no fear disturbs,
>   no hope seduces,
> But everything works to the praise of
>   and delights in the Son of God.
> There day utters speech to day,
>   and I long to utter it to you, young people,
>   but this matter is too high for me
>   and beyond your capacities.
> Yet on that day of triumph in the height of Heaven,
> when everyone is a child of day and Day itself,
>   'Day will utter speech to day'
> One day crying to another:
>   'In the beginning was the Word'
>   and
>   'The Word was made flesh'.[36]

It is easy to miss this poetical description of the praise of the Word and the joys of heaven whilst reading the text. Like many lovely things John has written, they need to be sought out and relished.

36. 34.2 (3:63).

The Word Made Flesh

The Word was made flesh for the cross. According to John, the cross, the complete sign of pain and suffering, is the *raison d'être* for the coming of Christ into the world. This forms the basis of John's Sermon 83: The Father's whole purpose in sending the Son into this world is that he might suffer and die for us. So, from the very first moment that the Word became flesh, he felt pain in this life.

John here takes up a tradition that is not likely to be accepted today, I suppose, though it is just possible that modern obstetrics would confirm the idea in a way John had not realized. The tradition is that Christ had full knowledge, as man, from the first moment of his conception, and therefore knew and experienced and actually felt the restrictions of his mother's womb. He was never lacking the sense of pain.[37] This gives another dimension to the phrase 'The Word was made flesh'—a dimension of pain that no other had suffered.

Yet paradoxically there was at the same time also great joy within the Word in his human nature. He became human in the first place because he delighted to be with us, one of us. This joy is communicated to us. We ourselves are enabled to enjoy real and true joy precisely because 'the Word was made flesh and dwelt among us.'[38] At that moment he became our Head. Because this fact gives meaning to our lives, because it is the only fact that *really* does give meaning to our lives, anyone who is seeking for the Word finds tremendous joy in contemplating 'the Word become flesh', and then 'and dwelt among us'.

John of Forde has a somewhat unusual interpretation of Saint John's text at this point. The text goes on: 'We have beheld his glory, glory as of the only Son from the Father' [Jn 1:14]. The obvious meaning is that the evangelist or the Apostles had seen Christ's glory shining in the face of Jesus. Not so John of Forde. No, the only eyes that are able to look on the glory of the Father's Only-Begotten are the eyes of Jesus himself. Therefore in this interpretation the phrase

37. 83.2 (6:2–3).
38. 25.6 (2:153); 94.5 (6:140–141).

'we have beheld' means that the eyes of Jesus have seen.[39] But I would hesitatingly suggest that he must mean that these eyes that see his glory are the eyes of the Whole Christ, Head and Body. Jesus' eyes are the eyes of the Church and also the eyes of the person who is a bride. At any rate, John seems to be talking about the Apostles who 'daily and almost continually contemplated the Only-Begotten', and this sight was still corporeal to some extent. They spoke with the Word, shared his home, lived his life, saw God in human form, face to face.[40]

Word and Church

This familiarity with the Word gives more strength to the two forms of love. The Church, or rather those in the Church who are worthy of the name Bride, never cease contemplating Jesus. They look at him either in the form of Wisdom and holiness and in the glory that is his as the only Son of the Father, or else in the form of lowly patience and humility that made him able to be born of his mother Mary.[41]

If this is true of the apostles, if it is true of Saint Paul, who saw the glory of God with unveiled face, then it is all the more true of Mary.[42] Among all the citizens of heaven—Thrones and Dominations and all the rest—there are none who have love and understanding equal to that of Mary. The love of the Mother of God was and is entirely unique; she loves God above all rational spirits. John of Forde sings her praises especially in Sermons 70 to 75.

John loves to quote the first three Chapters of Genesis, which deal with the origins and fall of humankind. He also loves to speak of the creation; rather, he loves to dwell on the Love that urged God to create the world—the Love that the Father had for the Son *before* he created the world: God's eternal love.

39. 16.1–2 (2:16–17).
40. 16.2 (2:17–18).
41. 61.9 (4:203–204).
42. 75.4 (5:158).

John forces us to think about the eternity before time, the ante-creation when God was (or is) God alone in the changeless simplicity of his Divine Nature. True to the principles of the great tradition of theology, John talks of the Trinity in Unity and the coequality of Persons.

> The Spouse is the Only-Begotten of the Father, and is loved by the Father as unique, as coequal, as consubstantial. I take it that the evangelist is indicating these aspects of love when he tells us: 'In the beginning was the Word and the Word was with God and the Word was God.'

He wants us to endeavour to contemplate 'the unfathomable mystery of the love within God's heart'.[43]

He was, of course, aware that we cannot grasp this Infinite Love. Only God can do that. But the effort on our part is not without use. To lift the mind and heart is sufficient in itself. To contemplate the mystery that 'the Word was with God' and how he, the Son, is in every way equal to the Father, is in itself enough to give an insight into the mystery of the Trinity. I do not know when I have read a more profound meditation of the Blessed Trinity than this Fourteenth Sermon of John of Forde's Commentary.

In another place he quotes the same text (Jn 1:1), but says that he would not presume to contemplate the Word in the beginning.[44] Yet he had done precisely this in the earlier sermon. We can, however, understand his hesitation, for this high contemplation of the Trinity is only open to those who fully and perfectly love the Blessed Trinity.

Freedom

I have already mentioned the theme of the Word coming into this world, the Word made flesh. The primary motive for his coming was that he was sent by the Father. The purpose was to do his Father's

43. 14.4 (1:255).
44. 97.7 (6:182).

will. Here we have ultimate freedom. In Sermon 65,[45] where he deals with the possible conflict between obedience and freedom, John of Forde teaches that the restrictions of obedience and discipline actually underpin our free choice and our chosen freedom. They serve the good of the community. Anyone who accepts the captivity of obedience becomes a truly free child of the truly free Jesus, whose freedom consisted in that he did not come to do his own will but the will of him who sent him [Jn 6:38]. Such obedience is: 'spontaneous, thoughtful, prompt, immediate, full of joy yet calm, patient, singleminded, powerful, not to be deterred.'[46] In other words, there is no lack of freedom in doing the Father's will. Rather, this is the real test of freedom. That is why Jesus says so eagerly, 'my food is to do the will of my Father'. He has no other *raison d'être*. There is just nothing stronger, nothing more free than this total surrender to the Father's will.

Eucharist

All this is associated with Chapter 6 of Saint John's Gospel, whose primary theme is 'the bread of life'. When, in 1208, the Interdict was imposed on England, John of Forde was saddened because the monastery was depleted of its goods to pay the king's levy, saddened because the sacraments were withheld from monks and lay people. The Interdict did not remove the Mass entirely from the monastery. Apparently, the monks were allowed to receive the eucharistic bread at least once a week, but they did not have it every day. Presumably this means that Mass was said every week in the monastery.[47] Outside, in the parishes, this was not the case. All the sacraments were withheld from the people and, at the time John wrote, this had been going on for two years—which dates Sermon Forty-one to 1210.

In another place John criticizes those monks who had become so involved in farm work, who were so taken up with cows and sheep

45. 65.11 (5:48).
46. 9.7 (1:186).
47. 41.7 (3:142).

and the cultivation of wheat that they had no time for recollection or the quiet of contemplation. In other words, those who were more interested in the bread of this earth which perishes than in the bread of heaven which endures to eternal life.[48]

Sermon Thirty-one was, possibly, written just before Easter. John says, 'Tomorrow is the true Passover', putting these words into the mouth of Moses as he comes down from the mountain. He quotes Saint John's Gospel here, for Moses points to Jesus in prophecy as if to say 'This is the Lamb of God who takes away the sins of the world.'[49] Again Moses takes up this theme of the Paschal Lamb who must die for our salvation.

> His fleece is truly a mantle, his flesh is truly food, and his blood is truly drink. Whoever covers himself with this fleece will not fear the coming of the winter cold, or the shame of being naked. Whoever makes his meal on this flesh will not dread hunger or disease. Whoever drinks this blood will not thirst or grow sad for all eternity'.[50]

This is the true keeping of the Passover. By this we become an Easter people. If that is true of the people of God as a whole, it is also true of the individual.

Christ nourishes the soul.[51] All who look on him with love are filled with complete satisfaction, for 'the flesh of Jesus is food indeed and his blood is drink indeed.' Clearly he has the Eucharist in mind, but his more immediate theme is the faith we express when we ruminate or ponder Christ's love and humility. These are the qualities that constrained him to become 'flesh' for our sake and to undertake in that same flesh the pain of his Passion. By meditating on his flesh and blood in this sense, we eat and drink them; rather we chew him and gulp him down. John tries to shock us with his language here: we go to this meal voraciously, we bite, we chew, we sup it down—the whole lot. 'With insatiable hunger—let me not call it a voracious

---

48. 89.9 (6:78).
49. 31.2 (3:25–27).
50. 31.3, quoting Jn 6:54 (3:29).
51. 8.2 (1:163).

maw—we devour his flesh and lap his blood',[52] like eaglets tearing
the flesh of their prey and sucking up its blood. Crude imagery to
express a spiritual thought—but always in the background there is
Saint John's Gospel.

In reality John of Forde wants us to lift our hearts to a higher
plane of reality, to go beyond the human nature of Christ. This is
still flesh. Those who love Christ simply in his human nature have
not yet attained the love of him in his divine nature. They have to
learn how to love him spiritually. 'It is the Spirit that gives life, the
flesh does not profit at all',[53] he says, borrowing from Saint John a
passage that was used often by Saint Bernard and the other writers
of the twelfth century.

JESUS AND THE FATHER

I have tried to give some idea of John's use of the Fourth Gospel,
particularly the early chapters. I would now like to turn to the
Last Supper chapters in order to make some observations on the
relationship between Jesus and his Father whom we call God.

In Sermon Nine John meditates on the thoughts about God that
arise in the heart of Jesus. He groups these as humility, reverence,
obedience, and praise or thanksgiving. When talking of reverence, he
quotes Saint John, Chapter 6, to show that in the heart of Jesus there
resides that supreme wisdom which makes us no longer disciples of
men but persons taught by God [Jn 6:45]. Likewise the obedience of
Jesus is demonstrated when Saint John's Gospel says' 'My food is to
do the will of my Father that I may perfect his work [Jn 4:34]'. This
is not a constrained obedience, not mechanical, but spontaneous,
joyful, and pleasant. It also has continuity: 'Whatever pleases the
Father, I continue to do always [Jn 8:21]'.[54]

After this he discusses briefly Jesus' thanksgiving—how devoted
he was to the glory of the Father-Creator. It is as if John wanted

52. 8.2 (1:163).
53. 48.6 quoting Jn 6:64 (4:22). Cf. Saint Bernard, *On the Song of
Songs*, 10.5; (CF 4:66); 33,2 (CF 7:146); Guerric of Igny,'Third Sermon for
the Annunciation', 6, *Liturgical Sermons*, Vol 2 (CF 32:53); 47–54.
54. 9.5, 7 (1:184–185, 187).

112

to make a psychological study of Christ's mind, choosing, not the categories of, say, the Myers-Briggs jungian assessment, but the ancient christian categories. Certainly praise would be one of these. The heart of Christ gives praise to the Father for the whole of creation, taking it into a spacious universal hymn of praise. Even when he thinks in his own words, Jesus keeps these totally free of self: 'The words I speak, I do not speak of myself. My Father who dwells in me does the work' (Jn 14:10). In other words,

> All the graces flowing in great rivers to their fountain-head, namely, the wellspring of the Father's glory, come pouring back with the selfsame power on him whom we confess and shall for eternity confess.[55]

The Church as the Body of Christ must also join in his praise. After the Ascension, when Christ remains in glory with the Father, he has departed from us. Even so, the Church is not left desolate. Often enough she grows tepid. There is no spark within her. The fire needs to be rekindled, that is to say, she needs not only to start with love and praise, but to remain constantly with it. 'Abiding in love' [Jn 15:10] means persevering in it, says John: 'He is speaking here of "abiding", that is, of persevering in love'.[56] The wood is laid on the fire, the flame begins to glow, and then the bonfire bursts into huge blazing flames, when the Father and the Son come into the heart of the Church, 'We shall make our home with him'—so that love will never ever fade.[57]

Equality with the Father

John was by no means a scholastic theologian, and nobody should look for a systematic presentation of theology in his sermons. His teaching is theologically competent, however. More than that, it is splendid and original. This is seen very clearly in Sermon Fourteen,

55. 9.8 (1:188).
56. 103.9 (7:39).
57. *Ibid.*

to which I have already referred. It is almost a treatise on the Trinity. Coming near the beginning of these one hundred twenty sermons, it is a statement of belief and at the same time a profound meditation on the most precious mystery of faith. It rests on the verse *Caput eius aurum optimum* [Sg 5:11]: His head is of finest gold—which should perhaps be translated 'His head shines brilliant like pure polished gold'.

John hesitated to talk of this mystery, but did so anyway. The two commandments of charity—love of God and love of neighbour—flowed from the fount of charity. He quotes Saint John's account of the last Supper: 'I know that the command of my Father is eternal life [Jn 12:50]'. He develops this by pointing out that God himself has practised these two commandments from the beginning, for the Father loved his only Son and the Son loved the Father. The Father loved the Son who was God—and therefore practised the love of God; and in loving him he loved his neighbour who was his Son.[58]

Glory

Thus this sermon is a profound meditation on the mystery of the unity and equality of the Three Persons in the Trinity, helping the reader to remain in deep silence before the Triune God. From this contemplation arises a need, but for us this is the glory: God's love is lavish towards the needy. Our response is to give glory in return. John here takes up the theme that he found in the Gospels:

> Since the love of these three for one another is so super-abundant, how could each not glorify the other with all his might? 'Father,' says the Son, 'glorify your Son, so that your Son may glorify you [Jn 17:1]'. Of the Holy Spirit likewise the Son says, 'He will glorify me when he comes [Jn 16:4]'. In all we do God is to be glorified; and yet how much more does God himself, who alone knows how deserving he is of every honour, owe befitting glory to his holy name? [59]

58. 14.1–2 (1:251–252).
59. 14.8 (1:262).

Everything therefore should be referred to the glory of God. That is why Jesus, when asked about the man born blind, said that it was to manifest the works of God [Jn 9:3]. And he attributed the death of Lazarus to the same end, namely 'for the glory of God, that the Son of God may be glorified in it [Jn 11:4]'.[60]

In this life the glory we must give to God is enveloped in shadow and darkness, as if we were being given a passing glance at what is in store or are taken up momentarily, as Paul was. When the wonderful daylight of eternity appears, there will no longer be need for shadows. Jesus will show himself openly face to face: 'I shall not then speak to you in parables, but I shall openly tell you of the Father.'[61] John has transferred the words of Jesus about the post-resurrection period to the next life. He does the same thing in an earlier sermon when he refers to the blessed vision of the saints in heaven who are worthy to hear the Father speaking openly of the the Son and the Son speaking of the Father.[62]

The same interpretation is found also in Sermon 72:6 where John is speaking of the final glory of the Church triumphant in heaven. But in Sermon Ninety-six it occurs as part of a wonderful hymn of praise that the Church, true Bride of Christ, sings to God concerning her future glory when she considers the words of the Song of Songs, 'There you will teach me'.[63] *There*. In heaven, where there will be luminous contemplation and blessed joy. There, all teachers will be silent while Jesus speaks quite openly of the Father.

Love

Yet even on this earth there can be some revelation of the Father's love. As a person becomes more united with Jesus, he or she is given a more intimate name. No longer 'servant' but now 'my Beloved'.[64] This is because he or she has been allowed to share in the secret

60. 14.8 (1:263).
61. 34.10 (3:70).
62. 19.5 (2:68).
63. 72.6 (5:125); 96.9 (6:174).
64. 47.5 (4:7).

thoughts of the Father. This is what is meant by friendship with God. Jesus has made known the things he heard from the Father [Jn 15:15], the secret of his Father's love, and in doing so he has established this friendship on a firm basis. He has drawn aside the veil that was hiding the joys of heaven and shown them, not to everyone, but to his friends.

In Sermon Seventy-five John applies these words in a very special way to the Blessed Virgin Mary. According to tradition, which he follows closely here, Mary had received from the Father a greater outpouring of grace than any other person in the whole of creation— including the angels. John mentions here three subjects of her contemplation: salvation, God's word, and God's promise. Mary was the person closest to Christ at the moment of the Incarnation and stood at the foot of the cross when he died for our salvation. John also implies that her son had revealed himself to her as God's Word, or at any rate as the Only Son of God, equal to the Father. The promise was given to her in a very special way, because whatever he heard from the Father he made known to us [Jn 15:15] and has written it on our hearts through the Holy Spirit.[65]

Returning to the Church, the Bride of Christ, John speaks of the extraordinary tenderness of Christ for his Bride, likening it to the tender and passionate love a man has for his wife. He has this to say in a passage that culminates in Chapter 15 of the Fourth Gospel:

> The Spouse himself is quite unable to conceal this tenderness from his Bride. He knows her not only as her Spouse, but he speaks to her as a Spouse, acts towards her in everything as a Spouse. If for the time being the full force of his charm remains hidden from the little ones, this is surely not so for the Bride. He comes forth from his Father, and whatever he has heard from his Father, he whispers intimately to his Beloved. What he has learnt in the bosom of the Father overflows into the bosom of his Beloved [Jn 13:25].[66]

65. 75.5 (5:159–160).
66. 29.2 (3:2–3).

In the place where John referred to the ineffable things spoken in an ineffable manner, he tells where Jesus has heard these things:

> He speaks of what he has heard from the Father, and in the manner he has learnt from the Father. What man is fit even to think of these things?' [67]

Departure

Whether John had some foreboding of his own death when he deals with the subject of death in Sermons One Hundred Five and One Hundred Six is difficult to say. It is hardly possible that he should speak of death so poignantly without considering his own. To be sure, he was anxious that he had not progressed very far in the spiritual life—that the 'old man' was still very much alive and ruled his life to an extent he did not like.[68] At the same time he looked forward to his own death, hoping that it would be precious and victorious with Christ's victory over death.[69] Temporal death breaks the sweet bonds of this bodily life, but God is the *fons vitae*, the fount of life, who gives us eternal life.

The theme of death receives a new twist in the final sermon, Christ's swan-song as he returns to his Father. The early Church in the person of the apostles, is filled with sorrow when Jesus warns of his immediate departure.[70] She cannot bear to see him depart. But when he explains in detail that he is going back to the bosom of the All-powerful Father, which is his own chosen place, and that he will send the Holy Spirit from there, then the mood changes. The early Church begins to rejoice because he is going to the Father (Jn 14:28). The point here is that the Church looks beyond present sorrow and begins to contemplate not only Christ in glory, but also her own eventual position with Christ in the same glory with the Father.

67. 21.7 (2:101).
68. 106.11 (7:75).
69. 106.10 (7:74).
70. 120.6 (7:246–247).

Elizabeth Oxenham, OCSO _____

The Return of the Jews at the End of Time in the Sermons of John of Forde
On the Song of Songs

IF I WERE ASKED to define the spirituality of the early Cistercians in one word, I would describe it as an Advent spirituality. The number of sermons they devoted to probing ever more deeply into the mystery of the coming of the eternal God into this world of time is ample proof of its paramount importance in their lives. We have only to recall Bernard's seven sermons dedicated to the season of Advent, for example, or Guerric of Igny's five sermons for the same season, to be aware of this. But there is another reason why their spirituality merits the name of an *Advent* spirituality: not only did our early Fathers look back in wonder and admiration to the Infant lying in a manger, they also looked forward with ardent longing to his return in power and majesty at the end of time. Their lives were lived in a constant tension between these two comings, between Bethlehem and the Parousia. As Guerric of Igny puts it, with a precision impossible to convey in translation: *sicut autem ecclesia in antiquis iustis expectavit adventum primum, sic in novis reexpectat secundum* (Just as the faithful of the Old Covenant longed for Christ's first coming, so now in the time of the new Covenant, they look forward to his second coming).[1]

---

1. Adv 1.2. Latin text in vol. 1 in the Sources Chrétiennes edition (Paris: Les éditions du Cerf, 1970). English text in *Liturgical Sermons*, vol. 1, Cistercian Father Series, no. 8 (1970).

117

In common with Bernard and Guerric and the other Cistercian Fathers, John of Forde in his sermons on the Song of Songs often meditates on these two Advents. Concerning the first coming, he speaks of pondering 'in tender love and happiness the child who is born for us, the little son who is given us' [cf. Is 9:6]; adding that 'no soul can be considered a true lover of Christ if she has not frequently kept watch to see the spouse coming forth from his bridal chamber'.[2] But it is in his reflections on the second coming that he shows himself at his most original. The frequency with which he links the Parousia with the pauline doctrine of the return of the Jews at the end of time, and the highly imaginative use of biblical imagery he employs to express this connection, is unique among the Cistercian Fathers. Although we certainly do find scattered references to the final salvation of the Jews in their writings—Bernard, for example, speaks of the Saviour returning 'to the place from which he had come, so that the remnant of Israel might be saved'[3]—nowhere do we find anything to equal John's passionate concern for, amounting almost to a pre-occupation with, their return. Aelred perhaps comes nearest to sharing his enthusiasm and his esteem for the jewish people, as he looks forward to the day when both Jew and Gentile will acknowledge 'one God, one faith, one baptism, and the Christians will welcome and embrace their Jewish brothers through charity, through solicitude and through affection'.[4] John could well have been giving a self-portrait as he described Saint Paul 'as if brimming over with the oil of gladness' when he reflected on the 'multiple predictions by the prophets that, at the end of time, the bride will seek for her former husband, for her King David.'[5]

Before we begin to explore the riches of John's thought on this subject, it is worth recalling that during his lifetime there were

2. Sermon 94.2 (6:136).
3. SC 79.5 (CF 40:142).
4. Sermon 15, *De oneribus*; PL 195:419. I am much indebted to Père Robert Thomas of Sept Fons for his informative study on 'Les cisterciens du 12ème siécle et les juifs'. This study was of great assistance in the preparation of this paper.
5. 66.2 (5:51).

increasing outbreaks of violence against the jewish community in many parts of England. The most notorious example of this violence occurred at York in March 1190, just a year before John's election as abbot of Forde. Almost the entire jewish community elected to end their lives in mass suicide rather than face almost certain death at the hands of the furious mob besieging York castle where the Jews had taken refuge. Indeed, the following morning, the few survivors who emerged, expecting clemency in return for christian baptism, were mercilessly massacred.[6]

We do not know John's reaction to this horrific event, or to the other outbreaks of anti-jewish violence, but from the appreciation he evinced for God's choice of Israel as his own people, we can be fairly certain his attitude would have resembled that of Saint Bernard when he came to the rescue of the Jews in the Rhineland, under attack from the angry mobs incited by the preaching of a renegade monk, Randolph. The contempt shown by Baldwin, archbishop of Canterbury—John's former abbot at Forde—towards a Jew who had accepted baptism under pressure and then recanted, dismissing him with the words, 'if he will not be a Christian, let him be the devil's man', would surely have saddened and perhaps even angered him.[7]

This is not to say that John was always positive in his approach to the jewish people, but when he does have some harsh things to say, he is only echoing, and sometimes embellishing, the laments and accusations of an Isaiah, a Jeremiah, or an Ezechiel. A good example of such embellishment occurs in Sermon 64, which is concerned with verse one of chapter seven of the Song of Songs: 'How beautiful are your feet in their sandals, O prince's daughter!' The mention of feet reminds him of Isaiah's description of Israel's arrogant behaviour and the fate that will befall her:

'Because the daughters of Zion are haughty and walk with outstretched necks, glancing wantonly with their eyes,

6. R. B. Dobson, *The Jews of Medieval York and the Massacre of March 1190* (York: St Anthony's Press, 1974) 27–28.
7. *Ibid.*, p.24.

mincing along as they go, tinkling with their feet, the Lord will strike with a baldness the heads of the daughters of Zion' [Is 3:16]. Alas, we see, and we groan over the shameful and longlasting baldness of Zion's captive daughters. True Justice has appeared in fleshly lowliness, and with the very sharp razor of judgment, in a moment shaved away all the fine qualities with which, independent of grace, she thought herself adorned. It is obviously the folly of this self-conceit that preceded the baldness, as if deserving and causing it, and this is what the prophet is telling us when he says: 'Because the daughters of Zion are haughty'. Because of this haughtiness, they do not proclaim and adore the glory of justifying grace, 'and they walk with outstretched necks', not seeking the help of grace and not giving thanks for helping grace. 'And they glance wantonly with their eyes', delighting with wanton folly in their own virtue, wherever they seem to be acting piously. 'And they mince along as they go, tinkling with their feet', doing everything to be seen by men, asking for every single step of their feet only the reward of glory that will pass away.[8]

The entire sermon is concerned with the long captivity of the Synagogue and her final return, and we shall be referring to it frequently in the course of this paper, because it contains so many of the themes which John associates with the final conversion of the Jews. It is this consistency in his approach to the subject that I find so impressive in what John has to say. Again and again the same themes recur, not only in the five sermons dedicated to the return of the Jews—Sermons 32, 62, 64, 66, 95—but also in the many other sermons which have related sections, some of them quite lengthy. This insistence on the same themes is never boring, both because of the wealth and beauty of the biblical imagery John employs, and because of the sheer artistry and skill of his development.

8. 64.4 (5:27).

He begins Sermon 64 by stating that 'the whole tune of this Song has as its principal and primary theme the most blissful and holy charity which joins and unites the Church, in the Holy Spirit, to her heavenly spouse', and he immediately goes on to add that 'the other bride is not to be defrauded of her praise, for she has been uniquely endowed with the gift of love, and dares to call the Lord of glory her spouse'.[9] John never envisages the destiny of God's chosen people in isolation, since both Jew and Gentile are called to enter into a bridal relationship with God; they are both tending towards a like end in the future: the coming, or the return, of the Messiah.

It is God himself who will bring about the reconciliation with his former wife, 'to whom in the past a bill of divorce was given'. This reconciliation with Israel will also be the means of restoring to her original form 'the bride who was gathered from the gentile nations. Already she is half-dead with cold, and he calls her back from her torpor to her first fervour.'[10] Here we touch on a fundamental aspect of John's teaching; it is perhaps his most original contribution. In his eyes this reconciliation is of crucial importance to the christian Church, since 'through Israel the christian faith will regain the strength of its former beauty, and love grown cold will regain its fervour.'[11]

The greater part of Sermon 62, from which this quotation is taken, concentrates on the renewal of the Church which will result from Israel's final conversion. To my mind, Sermon 62 is the most profoundly moving and exquisitely crafted sermon of the whole of John's commentary; it is a real masterpiece. He is commenting on verse twelve, chapter six of the Song of Songs: 'Return, return, O Shulamite; return, return, that we may gaze on you'. These words, he tells us, immediately

> strike a chord in the memory and demand our attention. They bring to mind the ancient story of Abishag, the Shu- lamite, who was sought 'throughout all the land of Israel'

9. 64.1 (5:24–25).
10. 64.2 (5:25).
11. 62.8 (5:8).

[1 Kg 1:3], when they were looking for a very beautiful girl who would keep David warm. He was then in his old age, very cold, and unable to find warmth in the clothes that covered him. So they brought this maiden to him, to stay at his side and keep him warm, and at night to sleep in his arms to keep him warm.[12]

While recognizing that these words describe an actual event, something that happened and is recorded in the Old Testament, John plunges deeper into the text to discover its eschatological significance:

. . . these are words from the distant past, and long ago their shadow passed away. The truth, though, that was faintly outlined beneath their veil, endures to this day, or rather, 'it will endure to eternity' [Dan 2:44], waiting for there to be a fulfilment of what is still held concealed within it, as if under a seal. Moreover, the chilly old age of King David, which could not be warmed by clothing, is an unmistakable portent of the state of the christian faith at the end of time. Christ, the true David, speaks openly of the coldness of those times, when he declares: 'Because wickedness is multiplied, most men's love will grow cold' [Mt 24:12].[13]

John takes comfort from the fact that despite the terrible inertia and tepidity which will afflict the Church at the end of time 'there will still be some who are faithful to our Lord, our "King David", and who are still animated by some little spark of charity, despite so great a coldness'. Their only recourse in this critical situation will be to follow David's example, and

to seek out for him the most beautiful maiden in the whole land of Israel, so that she 'may wait upon the king and be his

12. 62.1 (5:1).
13. 62.2 (5:2).

nurse; that she may sleep in his arms and warm our lord the king' [1 K 1:2]. What maiden is this? It is the people of Israel, whose first husband, God, will take thought to himself, remembering his youth, as Jeremiah says: 'I remembered you, pitying your youth' [Jer 2:2].[14]

The angels, too, the companions of the spouse, are concerned about the Church's inertia and loss of fervour.

'Christ is our David', they tell us, and here among his angels everything that is in him or within his orbit, takes warmth from him. From his face, too, there issues an impetuous stream of fire, inflaming all heaven with its charity, ravishing it with its goodness, intoxicating it with delight. Yet, on this frozen earth of yours, the head of Jesus 'is wet with dew, and his locks with the drops of the night' [Sg 5:2]. Down on earth he is a poor man, down on earth he is cold. He is weak there, he hungers and thirsts, he can scarcely find 'a place to lay his head' [Mt 8:20].[15]

The Church herself is acutely aware of her desperate need for Israel's return, 'your return is already all too necessary', she laments, addressing the Shulamite directly, 'for here on earth everything has already become lifeless and chill. Already the abyss of our sluggish tepidity calls out to the abyss of God's loving tenderness, the only direction from which we can be renewed.'[16] The intensity of her feeling is so great that she cries out with tears in her voice—*uoce igitur lacrimabili uotoque desiderabili*—reiterating again and again, 'Return, return, showing the loving goodwill of her petition as well as implying the very unhappy motive for her urgency and showing what an abundance of fruit she expects from her confidence.'[17]

14. 62.3 (5:3).
15. 63.5 (5:18–19). *Illic eget, illic alget, ibi languet, ibi esurit, et sitit.*
16. 62.10 (5:9).
17. 64.3 (5:25).

It is not her own need which impels the Church to plead with Israel to return.

> It is 'the Spirit of charity, which my beloved bestowed on me,' she tells us, which 'makes me feel compassion for the daughter of Zion. I pity her for giving my spouse a bill of divorce, that impudent and defiant step which she herself deliberately took in days gone by. But I rejoice with her to the full now that we see the day coming when the bill will be torn up. And the former bond will be renewed, as it was in the days of her youth [cf. Ezk 16:60], a new bond, "which will stand firm for ever". [Dan 2:44] When that day comes, I too shall go to meet her with exulting heart. I shall be there as a go-between to bring about a holy kiss, and in everything connected with her marriage bond I shall offer my help and mediation and testimony.'[18]

In this passage, taken from Sermon 30, as well as in the two previous passages from Sermons 63 and 64, John makes use of direct speech, a device he employs frequently to great effect. In this way the sense of drama is heightened, and the strong emotional content of the actor's words is enhanced. The audience, too, is given a feeling of immediacy, of being involved, in a way that indirect speech could never have achieved.

Sentiments such as these move the heart of the Spouse to turn his eyes again to the Shulamite, and he begins to recount 'what she will be like when she has begun to return, or rather, what she is already like in his eyes'.[19] For God, living in an eternal present, outside time, this reconciliation has already taken place, but John, living in time, and seeing no evidence of a change of heart in the Jews of his day, can have no inkling when this happy event will occur. Despite his deep concern, he does not bother with idle speculation about the actual time of Israel's return; that would be a futile exercise. His strong

18. 30.6 (3:20–21).
19. 64.3 (5:26).

faith in God's promises gives him the certainty that this happy and longed for reconciliation will take place:

> What your tender mercy has in store for the house of Israel, O loving Lord, Father of mercies, is hidden within your breast. The time of your good pleasure, the time when you take compassion on it, you know when it is, and you have it safely laid up in your treasuries. It is you who have control of it, and so it is something absolutely certain.[20]

Israel, too, experiences a like confidence and certainty about her eventual reconciliation: 'I read . . . that I have been written from the beginning on the palms of my Lord's hands [Is 49:16]. So I have an unshakeable faith in my complete reconciliation.'[21]

Instead, then, of wasting his energy on futile speculation about the exact time of Israel's conversion, John concentrates his attention on what he believes will characterise that festal day, 'a day longed for specially by the entire Church, when David will be brought back to Jerusalem with music of cymbal and song.'[22] He skilfully conveys the overwhelming joy that will inundate the hearts of both the spouse and the Church chosen from the nations on that day, by his use of verbs of physical movement, of running, of hastening. When Israel is still far off, the Church, in her impatience 'is already hastening forward to awaken in her an eagerness for the virtues that will be hers after so long a time.'[23]

Jacob, too, 'will run eagerly to embrace Joseph's son, so eagerly that he can scarcely contain himself for the inrush of overwhelming gladness.'[24]

Up till now, Israel herself has been unable to take even one step forward, wounded as she was in both feet through her overweening pride and self-reliance. But now that she has submitted herself to the

---

20. 32.1 (3:38).
21. 95:3 (6:152).
22. 23.8 (2:125).
23. 64.3 (5:26).
24. 95.4 (6:154).

grace of God and been healed, not only can she stand and walk, but she can run and leap, so that the bridegroom cries out in admiration: 'How beautiful are your feet in their sandals, O prince's daughter' [Sg 7:1]! Now

> you can run, and as grace increases, you can hasten your steps towards the end of the path, which is eternal life. You can leap, and come impetuously indeed, but happily, to the experience of those things which 'are above, with Christ' [Col 3:1], for grace bears you up.

But even leaping is not enough for John, as he searches for some way of describing the bride's ecstatic joy; ah, why not somersaulting?!— and we can almost hear him laughing as he pictures the bride turning 'somersaults with King David by leaping', since 'this is what is meant by walking among the things of heaven'.[25]

But it is the sight of her spouse running joyously to meet Israel, all her past offences forgiven, that causes the cup of her joy to overflow, as 'with a great cry of admiration he wipes away all tears from her eyes'.

> 'For a long time you were averted from me', he tells her, 'at last you have reverted to me; and now, you are wholly converted to me! With sudden and passionate swiftness you have redeemed all you had lost by your wretched slowness'.[26]

Diu nempe auersa, sero reuersa, sed iam plene conuersa es. In this succinct phrase John indicates another characteristic of Israel's return: namely, that 'the very tardiness of her salvation will be a very sharp spur to her late conversion, and the delay of so many centuries will be like a very happy shortcut to her on the way.'[27] 'The tardier

25. 64.5–6 (5:28–29).
26. 64.8 (5:30–31).
27. 95.12 (6:162).

that repentance, the more bitter; and the later, the more likely to be heartfelt.'[28]

John sees the fruit of Israel's repentance in her firm resolve to preach the Gospel, 'because she hopes in this way to be more fully reconciled to her husband, having herself become the reconciliation of "the full number of the gentiles' " [Rm 11:25].[29] She confides in her new-found husband her burning desire to make restitution by re-enkindling the faith of

> 'the church of the gentile people, which has been waiting for me until now. Though only at this late hour am I coming back to my right mind, the church has always summoned me to you, by your grace. This time I shall see to it that I repay so great a gift by planting you more profoundly in her heart, partly by the miracle of my conversion, and partly by the encouragement of my preaching and the proof I provide of your love. I shall be an arrow, piercing her heart with your love, or better, I shall be like a living mass of embers, ready to consume the hay and stubble among her wood'.[30]

There is no question, however, of Israel undertaking this mission of preaching by herself and on her own initiative. She is Abishag, and she works in close conjunction with King David, with Christ her king,

> and 'when he is seated in his teacher's chair, she will sit with him, to teach and instruct many nations. When he is walking also, she will run to and fro, "from one nation to another, from one kingdom to another people" [Ps 105:13], helping in the task of preaching. By building up these peoples, she will rejoice the heart of King David, as if with a glorious banquet of the best wine.' [31]

28. 32.1 (3:40).
29. 66.1 (5:50).
30. 95.9 (6:160).
31. 62.8 (5:8).

128

But the fruit of her preaching will not be the only wine Abishag offers her spouse. She also offers him spiced wine [cf. Sg 8:2], 'the wine of love which sorrow and sweetness have both spiced. For even if perfect love must cast out fear [cf. 1 Jn 4:18, RB 7:67], it does not cast out sorrow.'[32]

Over and above these two choice wines, there is yet another, the best. As at the marriage feast at Cana, Abishag will keep it till the last. For John sees her crowning glory, the sure proof of the absolute nature of her conversion, in the 'juice of pomegranates' [Sg 8:2], that is, the blood of her martyrs, which she joyously offers to Christ. This wine, however, is not spiced, since 'the very eagerness of her desire to suffer for Christ will not stoop to accept any admixture of grief. Far from it: the martyrs will run freely to the press, as if fermenting with new juice.'[33] Here again Israel shows how well she has learnt her lesson, that she cannot rely on her own strength alone to offer this supreme testimony of her love; as John puts it in his own poetic way, 'they will not be able to offer a drink like this to their spouse unless first they have been made drunk by him'.[34]

This mutual inebriation will be the prelude to the wedding banquet of heaven, where that other bride chosen from the gentile people will also celebrate her nuptials. 'It will be my delight to be present at that marriage', she tells us, 'where I trust that I too shall be inebriated to the last degree of joy. For at that marriage will be present my Lord Jesus, and for the nuptial day his cellars will be filled with wine.'[35]

John himself seems to have been given a foretaste of this inebriating cup, since much as he delighted to meditate on Christ's first coming at Bethlehem, he burned with even greater ardour as he looked forward to his second coming. For him, the return of Christ and the conversion of Israel were indissolubly linked together, and his heart overflowed with joy, as gazing into the distant future he beheld the two brides of Christ, Jew and Gentile, standing side by

32. 95.11 (6:161).
33. 95.12 (6:163).
34. *Ibid.*
35. 30.6 (3:21).

side and looking in the same direction as they cried out with one voice: 'Come, Lord Jesus' [Rv 22:20].

CONCLUSION

These extracts, chosen from among many scattered throughout John's sermons on the Song of Songs, and woven together, give some idea of his deep appreciation of Israel's chosen place in the economy of salvation. They also demonstrate his firm conviction that Israel's final conversion will be the means God will use to rekindle the fervour of the christian Church. Perhaps what impresses most of all is his unshakeable faith that despite all appearances to the contrary—especially in his day—God's salvific plan will triumph in the end: 'So great is the art and power of this master craftsman that no enemy, however strong, can have the slightest effect on him. Any malicious attempt to frustrate him, he seizes and wisely and powerfully bends it to his will and the adornment and service of his bride'.[36]

John's teaching is particularly relevant today, when Christians are becoming more conscious of their Jewish roots. His obvious love and concern for this people, dear to God, and therefore dear to him, provides us with both a stimulus and a challenge to deepen our knowledge and appreciation of our Jewish brothers and their rich spiritual heritage. The Second Vatican Council took a significant step forward in this direction in its decree on the Relationship of the Church to Non-Christian Religions. But even more exciting are the horizons opened up by a much neglected document brought out under the auspices of the Pontifical Commission for Religious Relations with the Jews in 1985, entitled, 'Notes on the Correct Way to Present Jews and Judaism in the Preaching and Catechesis of the Roman Catholic Church'.[37] If these Notes were given the study they

36. 67.13 (5:75).
37. This document was published in England under the title, *The Common Bond: Christians and Jews; Notes for Preaching and Teaching*, by the Catholic Media Office (1985). It is available from CMO Publications,

deserve, and if its recommendations were put into practice, the way would be open for a most fruitful dialogue and mutual co-operation between Christians and Jews.

This is how the document expresses the task that lies before us:

> Attentive to the same God who has spoken, hanging on the same word, we have to witness to one same memory and one common hope in Him who is the master of history. We must also accept our responsibility to prepare the world for the coming of the Messiah by working together for social justice, respect for the rights of persons and nations, and for social and international reconciliation. To this we are driven, Jews and Christians, by the command to love our neighbour, by a common hope for the Kingdom of God and by the great heritage of the Prophets.[38]

I can think of no better way of honouring John's memory and celebrating his abbacy at Forde than by pursuing this path.

Ashtead Lane, Godalming, Surrey. In the United States it was published under the title, *Notes on the Correct Way to Present Jews and Judaism in Preaching and Catechesis of the Roman Catholic Church*, by the United States Catholic Services, 1312 Massachusetts Avenue, N.W. Washington, D.C. 20005–4105. This edition has an excellent introduction prefacing the study.

38. *Ibid.*, p. 8.

Agrestis et infatua interpretatio:
The Background and Purpose of John of Forde's
Condemnation of Jewish Exegesis

IN SERMONS 31, 49 and 71 John of Forde leaves us in no doubt that he disapproves of jewish biblical exegesis. His most virulent condemnation appears in the first of these three sermons, where he speaks of the Jews as a wicked and adulterous generation (from Mt 12:39) who have refused to accept Christ. They have blocked the door to salvation with their false sense of security and their impenitent obstinacy, their shameless licence and their wilful impudence. They are impious, wicked, and dishonest. All unleavened bread tastes of Jesus (John is referring to 1 Cor 5:6–8), but the Jews have rendered it tasteless and useless with their 'wild lettuce',[1] their wild and ridiculous interpretation of scripture. But if the bread of doctrine does not taste of Christ, it does not taste at all! Every page of scripture proclaims Christ, but the blind and ignorant Jews refuse to see it.[2] Similarly, in Sermon 49, he speaks of *Israel secundum carnem*, whose share is nothing but the outward husk (*exterior cortex*). The Jew tastes it, but it does not attract him. He eats it, but it does not fatten him.[3] The Jew glories in the Law, but if the spirit does not give life, the letter kills.[4]

---

1. *Lactuca agrestis*: the normal translation of the Hebrew is 'bitter herbs' (Ex 12:8, Num 9:11). See John of Forde, Serm 31.6; ed. E. Mikkers and H. Costello, CCCM 17:248, 159–160 (ET 3:32).
2. 31.3–6; pp. 245–249 (3:27–35).
3. 49.1; p. 346, 10–13 (4:29).
4. 71.6; p. 499, 173–175 (5:115).

132

Such is John's poor opinion of the literal exegesis of the Jews. And it is clear that his opinion of the Jews themselves is not much better. He speaks of them as plotting Christ's execution;[5] he draws attention to their lack of faith;[6] and in his sixty-second sermon on Sg 6:12, *Revertere, revertere, Sulamitis!*, he dwells on what joy there will be both in heaven and on earth when the Synagogue returns to the one, true Church.[7] Much of this is fairly standard material, and the opposition of Church and Synagogue was a common iconographic theme.[8] By John's time the earlier, moderately tolerant attitude to the Jews and Judaism which we see in Gilbert Crispin's *Disputatio* had, for the most part, hardened and become much more embittered,[9] and there is nothing unusual in John's accusations of stubbornness, infidelity, hard-heartedness, obstinacy, and blindness to what the scriptures were obviously (for him) foretelling. Indeed, the patristic writers in general had equated *sensus Judaicus* with *sensus litteralis*,[10] essentially because of the Jewish 'refusal' to interpret the prophets christologically. And John's reference to the *exterior cortex* to which the Jews restricted themselves echoes Bernard's comment in his letter

5. 57.8; p. 404, 180–181 (4:147).

6. *Ibid.* lines 187–191 (4:147).

7. 62 *passim*; pp. 435–441 (5:1–13). See the discussion by Sister Elizabeth, pp. 117 to 130 above.

8. See P. Hyams, 'The Jewish Minority in Medieval England,' *Journal of Jewish Studies* 25 (1974) 278–279. Literary disputations between the Church and the Synagogue are to be found from the fifth century to the twelfth: see, for example, A. L. Williams, *Adversus Judaeos* (Cambridge 1935) 326–338, 381–383.

9. The best account of the changing attitudes of Christians to Jews during the course of the twelfth century is in Hebrew: A. Funkenstein, 'Hatemuroth bovikuach hadath sheben Yehudim leNotzrim bemeach hashnem asar' [Changes in Christian Anti-Jewish Polemic in the Twelfth Century], *Zion* 33 (1968) 125–44. In English see R. W. Hunt, 'The Disputation of Peter of Cornwall Against Symon the Jew,' in R. W. Southern (ed.), *Studies in Medieval History Presented to F. M. Powicke* (Oxford, 1948) 146–147, and Williams, *Adversus Judaeos*, 375–407. A critical edition of Crispin's *Disputatio* is now available in *The Works of Gilbert Crispin*, ed. A. S. Abulafia and G. R. Evans, *Auctores Britannici Medii Aevi* 8 (Oxford, 1986).

10. See R. Loewe, 'The Jewish Midrashim and Patristic and Scholastic Exegesis of the Bible,' in K. Aland and F. L. Cross (eds.), *Studia Patristica* 1: 492–514 (*Texte und Untersuchungen* 63; Berlin, 1957).

to Henry Murdac, written around 1130, where he encourages Henry to abandon his studies and enter the cistercian *schola pietatis*: '*O si semel paululum quid de adipe frumenti, unde satiatur Ierusalem, degustores! Quam libenter suas crustas rodendas litteratoribus Iudaeis relinqueres!*[11] Similarly, in the *Disputatio* against Symon the Jew, completed in 1208 (six years before the death of John of Forde), Johns' contemporary, Peter of Cornwall, spends the first six chapters of his second book attacking the literal interpretation of the Old Testament by his jewish opponents.[12]

In short, neither John's epithets for the Jews, nor his references to husks or crusts, nor his attack on their literal exegesis is particularly unusual, yet a reading of his thirty-first sermon leaves us in no doubt that he had very strong feelings on the subject and was prepared to express these feelings with considerable vehemence. Such vehemence, in fact, that some thirty years ago Christopher Holdsworth was led to observe that John 'denounced the Jewish understanding of the Bible at such length and with such fury as to make it likely that he was attacking a devotion to it among contemporary Cistercians.'[13] To what extent was this comment true? To what extent may John's condemnation of *agrestis et infatua interpretatio* be seen as a specific comment on tendencies within his own Order rather than a comment on the general tendencies of his times? We may begin our investigation by distinguishing between an interest in Hebrew and an interest in hebraic exegesis.

There is a myth in circulation that the Cistercians had 'a tradition of interest' in hebrew scholarship,[14] and 'showed an open interest in

11. Bernard of Clairvaux, *Ep.* 106.2; SBOp 7:266, 14–15. See also B. Smalley, *The Study of the Bible in the Middle Ages* (2nd ed. Notre Dame, 1964) 173, and J. Leclercq in G. W. H. Lampe (ed.), *The Cambridge History of the Bible 2: The West From the Fathers to the Reformation* (Cambridge, 1969) 191–192. For Bernard, the true study of the scriptures can only be achieved 'in the Church, through living participation in the tradition and prayer of the *Catholica*, in the spiritual atmosphere of the celebration of the liturgy and the assiduous study of the Fathers' (192).

12. See Hunt (n. 9) 146.

13. C. Holdsworth, 'John of Ford and English Cistercian Writing 1167–1214; *Transactions of the Royal Historical Society*, 5th ser. 11 (1961) 127.

14. B. Smalley, 'A Commentary on the *Hebraica* by Herbert of Bosham,' *Recherches de théologie ancienne et médiévale* 18 (1951) 33.

the study of Hebrew.'[15] Yet the evidence for this assertion is limited to two names: Stephen Harding and Nicholas Maniacoria. It is well known that the former, with the help of certain Jews in Northern France (for he himself could not read Hebrew), attempted to produce a more correct version of the Old Testament firmly established on the *Hebraica veritas*.[16] He completed his work by 1111, and the results survive as the four magnificent volumes of Dijon, *Bib. mun.*, MSS 12–15.

Maniacoria, who was more learned but more obscure, was a protégé of Queen Constance of Sicily. He was originally a Roman deacon of the church of Saint Laurence *in Damaso*, but towards the end of his life he retired to the cistercian monastery of Saint Anastasius *ad Aquas Salvias*, commonly known as Tre Fontane. Whether he died there or whether he went on to be appointed cardinal-deacon is unclear.[17] He had composed, he tells us, a revision of the Bible from which many superfluities had been removed, but the manuscript has vanished and all that remains are his *prolegomena* to the edition, the *Suffragenus bibliothecae*.[18] He has also left a *Libellus de corruptione et correptione Psalmorum* and one or two

15. A. Graboïs, 'The *Hebraica Veritas* and Jewish-Christian Intellectual Relations in the Twelfth Century,' *Speculum* 50 (1975) 618.

16. The term *hebraica veritas* derives from Jerome and is of fairly frequent occurrence: for its significance, see Graboïs (n. 15) *passim*, and W. McKane, *Selected Christian Hebraists* (Cambridge, 1989) 1–10. For Harding's contributions, see J. Martin, *Saint Étienne Harding et les premiers recenseurs de la Vulgate latine, Théodulfe et Alcuin* (Amiens, 1887), and the brief discussion in *The Cambridge History of the Bible*, 143–4. For the date of his Bible see Yolande Załuska, *L'enluminure et le scriptorium de Cîteaux au XIIe siècle* (Cîteaux, 1989) 66–69.

17. See A. Wilmart, 'Nicolas Manjacoria, Cistercien à Trois-Fontaines,' *Revue Bénédictine* 33 (1921) 136–46. A more recent bibliography is provided in E. Brouette *et al.*, *Dictionnaire des auteurs cisterciens* (Documentation cistercienne 16; Rochefort, 1975–1977) 523–524.

18. See J. Martin, *Introduction à la critique générale de l'Ancien Testament* (Paris, 1887) 1:cii–cviii, and H. Denifle, 'Die Handschriften der Bibel-Correctorien des 13. Jahrhunderts,' *Archiv für Literatur-und Kirchengeschichte des Mittelalters* 4 (1888) 270–276. The sole surviving manuscript is Venice, *Marciana* X 178 (Lat. X 279) ff. 141–181. For Maniacoria's statement that he had removed many superfluities, see Wilmart (n. 17), 139.

other works,[19] but none of them is well represented—none survives in more than one manuscript—and it is doubtful that they were ever well read.

Personally, I do not think that two names make a 'tradition', and we must also remember three other factors. Firstly, it is unclear as to how long Maniacoria was a Cistercian. He could not have entered Tre Fontane before 1140, since prior to that date the abbey was Benedictine, and Wilmart has suggested that he died about 1150.[20] It is therefore possible that Maniacoria was a member of the Order for only the last two years of his life and that his interest in biblical and hebraic studies had developed quite independently of the Cistercians. Secondly, neither the work of Harding nor that of Maniacoria had any significant influence on the version of the Bible used by the Cistercians. Harding certainly intended his Bible to be the standard for the Order,[21] but Bernard used the Vulgate, and what was good enough for Bernard was good enough for his followers. Harding's work might have been esteemed and treasured, but it was little used. Thirdly, between the death of Maniacoria in c. 1150 and the work of Giulio Bartolocci in the seventeenth century, we have no clear evidence of any Cistercian evincing an interest in Hebrew, and if hebrew studies were being pursued in cistercian monasteries, they were extraordinarily well concealed.[22]

19. See *Dictionnaire* (n.17), 523–524, F. Stegmüller, *Repertorium Biblicum Medii Aevi* (Madrid, 1950–1980) nos. 6003–6004, and Wilmart, *passim*. The *Libellus* has been edited by V. Peri, ' "Correctores immo corruptores." Un saggio di critica testuale nella Roma del XII secolo,' *Italia medioevale e Humanistica* 20 (1977) 19–125.

20. See Wilmart, 143.

21. See R. Loewe in *Cambridge History*, 143–144.

22. For Bartolocci, see *Dictionnaire* (n.17) 88. The *Encyclopaedia Judaica* (Jerusalem, 1971) 8:21-67 lists some 1400 christian Hebraists of whom only five are Cistercian: Harding, Maniacoria, Bartolocci, Carlo Imbonati (1650–1696), and Johann Berhard Venusi (1751–1823). An obscure Honorius (fl. 1452) may have been Cistercian, but that is uncertain. B. Altaner, 'Zur Kenntnis des Hebräischen im Mittelalter,' *Biblische Zeitschrift* 21 (1933) 288–308, lists over forty names from Paschasius Radbertus to Manuel Kalekas (*ob.* 1410), but Harding is the sole Cistercian. For other lists see P. E. Lapide, *Hebrew in the Church* (Grand Rapids, 1984) 207, n.44.

In any case, dissatisfaction with the various versions of the Jerome/Alcuin Vulgate and a demand for a sound and uniform text of scripture were fairly widespread.[23] The Cistercian Statutes of '1134' required *uniformitas* in liturgy and, *ipso facto*, in the text of substantial portions of the Bible,[24] and somewhat later, in the early thirteenth century, we see the development of the so-called 'Paris text' (together with the still later *correctoria*) which, as Raphael Loewe observes, 'was a natural growth that arose to meet the needs of the masters and scholars of the Paris Schools.'[25] If Harding and Maniacoria were part of a tradition, it was not a tradition which was specifically Cistercian.

Other evidence for cistercian interest in Hebrew is fragmentary, to say the least. There is a hebrew translation (in latin transcription) of the Apostles' Creed and the *Magnificat* in a twelfth-century manuscript from Kaisheim,[26] and there is the fact that when Herbert of Bosham, perhaps the best hebraist of the twelfth century, retired to a monastery at the end of his life, he chose the cistercian abbey of Ourscamp.[27] There he completed his remarkable commentary on the Psalter (which undoubtedly utilized jewish sources[28]) and dedicated the work to a former cistercian abbot, Peter, bishop of

23. See Loewe in *Cambridge History*, 140–145, and Graboïs, 'Hebraica Veritas,' 617 (citing the case of Sigo of Saint-Florent).

24. J. M. Canivez, *Statuta Capitulorum Generalium Ordinis Cisterciensis* (Louvain, 1933) 1:13: 'Missale, epistolare, textus, collectaneum, graduale, antiphonarium, regula, hymnarium, psalterium, lectionarium, kalendarium, ubique uniformiter habeantur.'

25. Loewe, in *Cambridge History*, 147.

26. Clm 7955 (Kaisheim 55) fo. 154v: see Lapide, *Hebrew in the Church*, 11–13.

27. See Smalley, 'Herbert of Bosham', 34–35. Further on Herbert, see Smalley, *Study*, 186–195, R. Loewe, 'The Mediaeval Christian Hebraists of England: Herbert of Bosham and Earlier Scholars', *Trans. Jewish Historical Society of England* 17 (1951–1952) 225–249, and *idem*, 'Herbert of Bosham's Commentary on Jerome's Hebrew Psalter,' *Biblica* 34 (1953) 44–77, 159–192, and 275–298.

28. See Smalley, 'Herbert of Bosham', 47–55 and Loewe, 'Christian Hebraists', 242–244.

Arras, who had at one time been abbot of Pontigny and then of Clairvaux.[29]

Aryeh Graboïs takes this information on Herbert, reminds us of the work of Harding and Maniacoria, and asks rhetorically: 'Did [Herbert] have at his disposal at Ourscamp a library of Jewish works or was he using notes already taken at Paris during the years of his studies?'[30] The answer to the first part of the question is undoubtedly No. But why, then, did Herbert retire to Ourscamp and why did he dedicate his work to Peter? Beryl Smalley has provided the answers to both questions. As to the first, Ourscamp 'was a natural choice for a former partisan of Becket. The Cistercians had supported the cause of Alexander III in his struggle with the Emperor. The abbot and monks of Pontigny had received Becket after his quarrel with King Henry. They had been all kindness and sympathy for the exiled archbishop and his *familia*.'[31] As to the second, it seems that Peter of Arras was 'acting as Herbert's spiritual director and in this capacity advised him to enter religion or else to undertake some teaching or writing.'[32] Peter, in any case, had some reputation for promoting scholarship.[33] In short, since Herbert intended to retire somewhere, it was only natural that he would choose a cistercian abbey and equally natural that he would dedicate his last work to his friend and spiritual director.

As for the other evidence adduced by Graboïs—that there were copies of a Hebrew-Latin glossary at Clairvaux (one of the them attributed to Stephen Langton)[34]—Graboïs is obviously unaware that glossaries of this nature were common and widely distributed. That by Langton alone survives in some three dozen manuscripts,

29. See *Gallia Christiana* (Paris, 1725, repr. Farnborough, 1970) 3:328–329 and 431–432.

30. Graboïs, 'Hebraica Veritas', 631.

31. Smalley, 'Herbert of Bosham', 34.

32. *Ibid.*, 32–33.

33. See the poem by Lambert of Saint-Vaast printed in *Histoire littéraire de la France* (Paris, 1869) 15:94.

34. Graboïs, 'Hebraica Veritas', 630.

and these come from all sorts of places, not just cistercian houses.[35] In any case, brief Hebrew-Latin glossaries are frequently found appended to copies of the Bible.

What, then, of the Kaisheim translation of the Apostles' Creed and the *Magnificat*? This can be regarded as no more than a curiosity, and its purpose was presumably related to jewish conversions to Christianity rather than to christian interest in Hebrew.[36]

We must also remember that there is one piece of evidence which may well indicate a cistercian distrust of hebrew scholarship. The General Chapter in 1198 decreed that a monk of Poblet who had learned hebrew letters from a Jew should be committed to the abbot of Clairvaux for correction,[37] but as Beryl Smalley points out: 'It is not stated that the monk in question was aiming at Bible study. Hebrew letters could also be used for casting magic spells.'[38] Smalley's comment is perfectly true: Hebrew letters could be used in this way[39] and Cistercians did occasionally lapse into dubious

35. See Stegmüller, *Repertorium*, nos. 7707–7709.

36. See Lapide, *Hebrew in the Church*, 7–19. The most common text translated into Hebrew at this period was, understandably, the *Pater noster*.

37. Canivez, *Statuta* 1:227: 'De monacho Populeti qui a quodam iudeo litteras hebraicas didicisse dicitur, abbati Claraevallis committitur ut inquirat et corrigat'.

38. Smalley, *Study*, 81, n.2.

39. Cfr. Loewe, 'Christian Hebraists', 226–227: 'A mystic spirit surrounded the weird shapes and names of the Hebrew letters . . . The mysterious, almost numinous quality of these letters rested upon the assumption that as the vehicle for God's first revelation of Himself to the Jews they possessed some occult symbolism—a spell under which the Jews themselves also fell.' Loewe points to the case of archbishop Gerard of York (d. 1108) who owned two Hebrew Psalters and had a reputation for both learning and magic. 'It must remain an open question', he remarks, 'whether his interest in Hebrew may not have been due to the cult of Mephistopheles rather than of the Muse' (*ibid.*, 234). See also Lapide, *Hebrew in the Church*, 155. Greek letters could be used in a similar way: see R. Merrifield, *The Archaeology of Ritual and Magic* (London, 1987) 137–138. On the other hand Gerard's Psalter was used as a source from which Maurice of Kirkham copied out forty Psalms when he was *adolescentulus*: cf. M. R. James, 'The Salomites,' *Journal of Theological Studies* 35 (1934) 287–297. I am indebted to Dr Christopher Holdsworth for this last reference.

pursuits.[40] But if the statute does not say that the monk was 'aiming at Bible study', neither does it say he was suspected of sorcery, and I think it far more likely that the monk in question was being rebuked for wasting his time (in monastic terms) in studying Hebrew when he should have been getting on with his prayers and *lectio divina*. In my own view, this statute probably indicates precisely what it appears to indicate: namely, that by the end of the twelfth century hebrew studies, far from being promoted, were actively discouraged in cistercian monasteries.

In summary, then, there is little to support (and some evidence against) a 'cistercian tradition' of hebrew biblical scholarship. All that we can say of Harding and Maniacoria is that they were Cistercians who had an interest in Hebrew, and there is nothing in the other evidence to persuade us that the Cistercians had a significantly greater interest in the language than many others of their day.

In any case, Harding and Maniacoria were interested only in the establishment of a better biblical text. Their interest in jewish exegesis, so far as we can tell, was nil. But what John of Forde is attacking is hebraic exegesis, not Hebrew, and we must therefore return to the question of why he felt so deeply on the subject. In this case, let us begin our investigation not with the Cistercians in particular, but with the twelfth and early thirteenth centuries in general. We must, of course, begin with Hugh of Saint-Victor who established the victorine principle that the historical-literal sense of scripture is a necessary and secure foundation for the allegorical.[41] *Lectio divina* was just as important for Hugh as it was for Stephen Harding or Bernard, but with Hugh the emphasis has been changed.[42] Hugh's own knowledge of Hebrew was shaky at best and his source for rabbinic exegesis was discussion with contemporary rabbis. They, as might be expected, provided him with

40. See D. N. Bell, 'A Cistercian at Oxford: Richard Dove of Buckfast and London, B.L., Sloane 513', *Studia Monastica* 31 (1989) 77–78.
41. See Smalley, *Study*, 86–106 and H. H. Glunz, *History of the Vulgate in England* (Cambridge, 1933) 249–250.
42. See Smalley, *Study*, 86–88.

interpretations which reflected the 'rationalist school' of Rashi and his followers (especially Joseph Kara, Samuel B. Me'ir [Rashbam], and Joseph B. Isaac Bekhor Shor[43]), and it was these ideas which Hugh transmitted to his disciples Andrew and Richard.

It is unnecessary to dwell at length upon the victorine achievement; the work of Beryl Smalley still remains fundamental,[44] and the capabilities and contributions of Andrew have been examined more recently in an excellent study by William McKane.[45] Andrew's own student, Herbert of Bosham, has already been mentioned,[46] but Andrew's influence was not restricted to his own pupils (and we know he had pupils[47]) nor to a small handful of selected followers. His name appears as one of the *auctoritates* in the *Registrum librorum Angliae*,[48] and we are told that his works were to be found in the augustinian priory of Guisborough and in Gloucester Cathedral.[49] The *Catalogus de libris autenticis et apocrifis* of Henry of Kirkstede offers a much longer list of his *opera* and adds to their locations the benedictine abbey of Bury Saint Edmunds and the cistercian abbey of Newminster.[50] As to surviving manuscripts, we know of eighteen, of which four come from the cistercian houses of Beaupré de Beauvais, Eberbach (near Mainz), and Buildwas and Kingswood in England.

43. On Joseph Kara, see *Encyclopaedia Judaica* 10:759–760; on Rashbam, *ibid.*, 14:809–812; on Joseph Bekhor Shor, *ibid.*, 4:410–411. See also n. 85 below.

44. See Smalley, *Study*, 83–195.

45. See McKane, *Selected Christian Hebraists*, 42–75.

46. See n. 27 above.

47. Andrew himself, Richard of Saint-Victor, Herbert of Bosham and Roger Bacon all testify to this; see Smalley, *Study*, 174–175 and *idem*, 'Herbert of Bosham', 64.

48. See Oxford, Bod. Lib., ms Tanner 165 fo. 117. The works listed are *Super vetus testamentum* (at Gloucester), and *Super Ecclesiasten, Super Parabolas*, and *Super Genesim ad litteram* (at Guisborough).

49. Neither of these manuscripts has been traced.

50. See R. H. Rouse, *Catalogus de Libris Autenticis et Apocrifis: A Critical Edition* (Cornell Univ., Ph.D., 1963) 1:72–73. Listed here are commentaries on Genesis, Exodus, Leviticus, Numbers, Deuteronomy, Joshua, Judges, Kingdoms, Chronicles, Ecclesiastes, Proverbs, Isaiah, Jeremiah, Daniel, and Joel. The commentaries on Isaiah, Jeremiah and Daniel were at Bury Saint Edmunds (now Cambridge, Pembroke College, ms 45), and those on Exodus, Leviticus, and Numbers at Newminster (the manuscript has not survived).

The others come from a whole variety of orders: Victorine (four), Augustinian, Dominican, Franciscan, Benedictine, and Carmelite.[51] We also know of lost collections from Saint Benet's College in Cambridge. the Benedictines of Melk, the Dominicans of the convent of Minerva in Rome, and (possibly) the Premonstratensians of Dryburgh Abbey in Scotland.[52] Still more important is the *Nachlaß* of Andrew as it appears in later and greater names: Peter Comestor, Peter the Chanter, and Stephen Langton, but that is a matter we shall discuss in its proper place. In short, there is no doubt that, as Smalley say, 'Andrew's works aroused permanent interest'[53] and that his influence after his death was considerably greater than it had ever been during his lifetime.

It would be wrong, however, to suggest either that the Victorines were wholly responsible for the development of literal exegesis or that it was restricted to them. Smalley, again, draws our attention to an early twelfth-century commentary on the literal sense of Leviticus composed by an anonymous writer who makes no use of, and shows no knowledge of, either Hugh or Andrew of Saint-Victor.[54] That he consulted with Jews seems not in doubt and he 'show no signs of supposing that his procedure . . . is anything out of the ordinary.'[55] He had attempted, without great success, to learn some Hebrew[56]

---

51. See Smalley, *Study*, 175–178 and Stegmüller, *Repertorium*, nos. 1295–1329. To the list of manuscripts provided by Smalley must be added London, B.L., Royal 13 C.iv (from the Lincoln Carmelites), London, B.L., Harley 3225, and Salamanca, *Univ.*, ms 2061.

52. See Stegmüller, *Repertorium*, no. 1329 (Saint Benet's) and Smalley, *Study*, 176 (the Roman Dominicans and Melk). The case of Dryburgh is uncertain: Adam of Dryburgh certainly used Andrew's works (see Smalley, 'The School of Andrew of Saint-Victor,' *Recherches de théologie ancienne et médiévale* 11 [1939] 163 and *idem*, *Study*, 180–181), but we do not know where he found them.

53. Smalley, 'School of Andrew', 167.

54. *Idem*, 'An Early Twelfth-Century Commentator on the Literal Sense of Leviticus,' in B. Smalley, *Studies in Medieval Thought and Learning* (London, 1981) 27–48 (originally in *Recherches de théologie ancienne et médiévale* 36 [1969] 78–99).

55. *Ibid.*, 34.

56. See *ibid.*, 36. Pedagogical tools for learning Hebrew in the twelfth century were non-existent. There were only the Hebrew-Latin glossaries and a few phrase-books for pilgrims going to the Holy Land (see B. Bischoff,

and, as Smalley points out, he is 'a precious witness to the fact that biblical scholarship developed independently of Saint-Victor and in centres other than Paris.'[57] A similar unknown commentator produced literal glosses on the book of Job sometime after 1100,[58] and I do not think that there is any doubt that these brief passages predate the activity of Hugh of Saint-Victor.

More important and more persuasive, however, is the Leviticus commentary of Ralph of Flaix; not, in this case, because it presents a literal exegesis, but because it does not.[59] It was composed about 1150, it proved to be extremely popular, and it was written (as Ralph himself tells us) to deal with the problems that the simpler monks of his community were having in dealing with jewish ideas. 'A clear purpose runs through the twenty books . . . Ralph aimed first and foremost at refuting Jewish arguments for the benefit of his brethren at Flaix. The monks had been discussing among themselves the objections put forward by Jews.'[60] But the prologue to Ralph's commentary makes it clear that it was not always the Jews who were putting forth jewish arguments so persuasively: it was also christian religious![61] And there is no reason to assume that the topics so eagerly discussed at Flaix were not discussed with equal eagerness elsewhere. The very fact that Ralph's wholly allegorical commentary was to be found in so many monastic libraries may well reflect abbatial concerns about too deep a monastic interest in literal exegesis.

'The Study of Foreign Languages in the Middle Ages,' *Speculum*, 36 [1961] 218–219). The only effective way to learn the language, therefore, was by personal instruction, and there was no provision for teaching Hebrew in universities until the second decade of the fourteenth century: see Loewe in *Cambridge History*, 152.

57. See Smalley, 'Early Twelfth-Century Commentator,' 47.

58. See Smalley, 'Les commentaires bibliques de l'époque romane; glose ordinaire et gloses périmées,' in *Studies*, 19–21 (originally published in *Cahiers de civilisation médiévale*, IVe année [1961] 15–22). The manuscript in question is Oxford, Bod. Lib. Rawlinson G.17.

59. See B. Smalley, 'Ralph of Flaix on Leviticus,' in *Studies*, 49–96 (originally published in *Recherches de théologie ancienne et médiévale* 35 [1968] 35–82).

60. *Ibid.*, 66.

61. See *ibid.*, 67.

Still further evidence for a widespread interest in jewish interpretation may be found in the work of Honorius Augustodunensis.
Honorius was, above all, a popularizer, and in his *Imago mundi*,
composed in the early years of the twelfth century (the first recension
dates from about 1110),[62] we can see the distinct influence of rabbinic exegesis.[63] We must remember, too, that not only does the first
version of the *Imago mundi* predate Hugh of Saint-Victor, but that
it was extremely widely read (more than three hundred manuscripts
are known) and immensely influential.[64] Valerie Flint, therefore, was
led to suggest that a careful examination of Honorius's work reveals
that 'the teachings of the Jews may have had a deeper impact upon
the traditions, teachings and writings of medieval society than we
have even begun to recognise.'[65]

Rashi, after all, was living in Troyes in the second half of the
eleventh century (he died in 1105), and it is well known that at
that period and in that area Jews and Christians were on better
terms than at most other times and in most other places.[66] Nor was
the intellectual commerce all one way: Rashi and the other jewish
commentators were also affected by christian exegesis, though not
nearly to the same extent.[67] Similarly, in twelfth-century England

---

62. See M. O. Garrigues, 'L'oeuvre d'Honorius Augustodunensis: Inven-
taire critique,' *Abhandlungen der Braunschweigischen Wissenschaftlichen
Gesellschaft* 38 (1986) 29–30.

63. See V. I. J. Flint, 'Anti-Jewish Literature and Attitudes in the Twelfth
Century,' *Journal of Jewish Studies* 37 (1986) 39–57, 183–205.

64. See Garrigues, 27–33.

65. Flint, 'Anti-Jewish Literature', 193. Cfr. *ibid.*, 39–40: 'Rabbinic
exegesis, especially exegesis of the *Book of Genesis*, affected the approach
to the Bible of the ecclesiastical reformers more profoundly than many of
us have in general supposed.'

66. See generally the excellent study by Robert Chazan, *Medieval Jewry
in Northern France* (Baltimore, 1973), espec. 24–29, and E. Shereshevsky,
'Some Aspects of Everyday Life in Rashi's Times,' *Jewish Quarterly Review*,
65 (1974–1975) 100–101.

67. See Shereshevsky, 'Rashi and Christian Interpretations,' *Jewish
Quarterly Review* 61 (1970-1971) 76–86; Smalley, *Study*, 155–156. The
best example is perhaps Elhanan B. Yakar of London, who was 'well
acquainted with contemporary Christian theological works, both in Latin
and French, and included almost literal quotations from such works in his

'the fact of frequent meetings [of Jews and Gentiles] in the course of everyday life is established beyond doubt',[68] and although the church disapproved of any such consultations[69] and could take the severest measures against those who were so foolish as actually to convert to Judaism,[70] it seems that from the time of Anselm onwards Jewish-Christian discussions and jewish exegesis had become the fashion.[71] Hugh and Andrew of Saint-Victor may have refined the procedures, but they certainly did not invent the process. The bandwagon was already well on its way.

Anselm is also important for another reason: namely, for drawing our attention to the growing dissatisfaction with the idea of 'blind faith' which we see developing throughout the twelfth century.[72] Both Anselm and Abelard represent faith in search of understanding, and the claims of reason were to become even stronger when, in the second half of the century, the new translations of Aristotle set all Europe ablaze. And what was the end of all this? The hegemony

---

writings. In this he is unique, as far as is known, among theologians of the Hasidei Ashkenaz movement' (*Encyclopaedia Judaica* 6:613).

68. Hyams, 'Jewish Minority' (n.8), 274.

69. See S. W. Baron, *A Social and Religious History of the Jews* (New York, 2nd ed. 1957) 5:108–137. For further bibliography, see Smalley, 'Ralph of Flaix,' 67, n. 92, to which should be added S. Grayzel, *The Church and the Jews in the XIIIth Century* (New York, revd. ed. 1966) and J. A. Watt, 'The English Episcopate, the State and the Jews: the Evidence of the Thirteenth-Century Conciliar Decrees,' in P. R. Coss and S. D. Lloyd (eds.), *Thirteenth Century England: Proceedings of the Newcastle Upon Tyne Conference 1987* (Woodbridge, 1988) 137–147.

70. The standard examples are the anonymous deacon who was burned in 1222 (see F. W. Maitland, 'The Deacon and the Jewess,' in his *Collected Papers*, ed. H. A. L. Fisher [Cambridge, 1911] 1:385–400) and Robert of Reading who died in prison, still jewish, in 1275 (see R. Loewe, 'The Medieval Christian Hebraists of England: the *Superscriptio Lincolniensis*,' *Hebrew Union College Annual* 28 [1957] 210, with further bibliography in n.24).

71. For Anselm's discussions with Jews and their impact on his *Cur Deus homo*, see R. W. Southern, *Saint Anselm and his Biographer* (Cambridge, 1963) 88–91. Gilbert Crispin's *Disputatio* (n.9 above), was composed c. 1092–1093, just about the time Anselm became archbishop of Canterbury.

72. See Glunz, *Vulgate*, 198–200.

of the schools and the development of the university. As Raphael Loewe has observed: 'the reassessment of the value of literal(i.e. historical) exegesis must owe something to the fact that Theology was being promoted, at least in Paris, to the dignity of a discipline in its own right.'[73] The greater the claims for the autonomy of reason, the greater the emphasis placed on reasonable, literal exegesis. Not that this helped the Jews. Amos Funkenstein has pointed out that from the earlier standpoint of faith, they could be excused for failing to see that the Old Testament prophecies pointed to Christ. But now, from the standpoint of reason, their refusal to see this could only be considered as deliberate and unreasonable perversity.[74]

It seems to me, therefore, that the cumulative evidence of christian-jewish contacts, of the popularity of victorine exegesis, of the concern of Ralph of Flaix for his simpler and more gullible brethren, of the popular work of Honorius Augustodunensis, and of other similar matters leads us inexorably to the conclusion that an interest in jewish argument and exegesis was the rule rather than the exception in the twelfth century and that John of Forde's attack on its inadequacies was, from his point of view, both necessary and justified.

But what of the Cistercians? Is there any evidence that they were more interested in this type of exposition than their augustinian, benedictine, carmelite, dominican or franciscan colleagues? The answer is that there is indeed some evidence, but it must not be overrated. We have already mentioned that of the various manuscripts of Andrew of Saint-Victor, both lost and surviving, five were from cistercian houses, and we should note that of the two manuscripts of the anonymous commentary on Leviticus discussed above, one is from Eberbach.[75] On the other hand, five of Andrew's manuscripts were from benedictine houses (as also is the other manuscript of

---

73. Loewe, '*Superscriptio Lincolniensis*,' 205–206.
74. See Funkenstein's discussion cited n.9 above.
75. Now Oxford, Bod. Lib., ms Laud lat. 14 (for a description, see Smalley, 'Early Twelfth-Century Commentator,' 27–28). The other manuscript is from the benedictine abbey of Saint-Amand: now Valenciennes, *Bib.mun.*, ms 25 (described *ibid.*, 28).

the anonymous Leviticus commentary) and four were victorine; and given the wholesale destruction of english monastic manuscripts at the Dissolution and the still inadequate cataloguing of surviving biblical commentaries, it is dangerous to draw too firm a conclusion from somewhat shaky evidence. The Cistercians may have had a particular and unusual interest in Andrew's work, but we cannot be certain of this. What *is* certain is that an interest in jewish exegesis was widespread in the twelfth and early thirteenth centuries and there is no reason to suppose that the Cistercians were unaffected by the trends of the times.

It might be suggested that what we have said so far accounts sufficiently for John's comments. I do not think so. We may, perhaps, go one stage further and see in them not just an echo of prevailing interest in the *sensus judaicus,* but an allusion to the very reason for the existence of his long, diffuse, and (if I may say so) tedious commentary.

We mentioned above that Andrew of Saint-Victor undoubtedly had pupils, but that his greatest impact was not to be seen in such scholars as Herbert of Bosham, whose commentary on the Psalter was, for all its learning, fairly obscure, but in those giants of the 'biblisch-moralische Richtung':[76] Peter Comestor, Peter the Chanter, and Stephen Langton.

Comestor owed much to the victorine emphasis on the literal study of the scriptures and he borrowed extensively from Andrew.[77] He may also have consulted with Jews directly (he was, after all, Dean of Troyes in 1147 and Rashbam did not die until c. 1174), and according to Esra Shereshevsky, clear evidence of rabbinic exegesis can be seen in his *Historia Scholastica.*[78] Peter the Chanter, likewise,

76. See M. Grabmann, *Die Geschichte der scholastischen Methode* (Freiburg im Breisgau, 1911 [repr. Graz, 1957]) 1:476–501.

77. See D. Luscombe, 'Peter Comestor,' in K. Walsh and D. Woods (eds.), *The Bible in the Medieval World: Essays in Memory of Beryl Smalley* (Studies in Church History, *Subsidia* 4; Oxford, 1985), 109–129, espec. 111–112, citing the work of Smalley.

78. See E. Shereshevsky, 'Hebrew Traditions in Peter Comestor's *Historia Scholastica,' Jewish Quarterly Review* 59 (1968–1969) 268–289. That rabbinic exegesis can be seen in Peter's work is not in doubt, but where

mined the victorine lode and it is possible that he, too, consulted Jews in the preparation of his commentary on the Pentateuch. But whether he did or not, he, too, borrowed a great deal of jewish exegesis from Andrew of Saint-Victor.[79]

Stephen Langton, finally, also bears witness to the deep influence of literal exegesis. To some extent this is not surprising since Peter the Chanter may have been his *magister*,[80] yet Langton does not cite Andrew uncritically. His own interest in jewish exegesis had led him to consult with contemporary rabbis (though he disapproved of disputations with Jews)[81] and he was prepared to compare Andrew's interpretations with what he himself had learned and decide logically which seemed better.[82] He too, like Harding and Maniacoria before him, found the contemporary versions of the Vulgate unsatisfactory, and he, too, made efforts—albeit unsystematic[83]—at emendation, though his most signal and permanent contribution to biblical studies was in the new arrangement of chapters which appeared for the first time in the Paris text and which is substantially the same as that in use today.[84]

Langton's commentaries, heavily dependent on literal exegesis, were extensively copied and were obviously influential, though few modern scholars read them and fewer still appreciate them. Indeed, even to read them is difficult, for apart from the commentary on Chronicles, I know of none which is available in a critical edition and not one has been translated into any modern language.[85] We,

---

he found it is a different matter. This interesting article does not exhaust Peter's *latin* sources.

79. See the careful and judicious study by Gilbert Dahan, 'Les intérpretations juives dans les commentaires du Pentateuque de Pierre le Chantre,' in *The Bible in the Medieval World*, 131–155.

80. See F. M. Powicke, *Stephen Langton* (Oxford, 1928 [rpt. New York, 1965]) 30.

81. See Smalley, *Study*, 235, n.2.

82. See *ibid.*, 236.

83. See Loewe in *Cambridge History*, 148.

84. See Powicke, *Stephen Langton*, 36–39, and Loewe in *Cambridge History*, 147–148.

85. See Stephen Langton, ed. A. Saltman, *Commentary on the Book of Chronicles* (Ramat-Gan, 1978). In his important introduction, Saltman

it seems , prefer to wander among the fleecy and amorphous clouds of allegory rather than to walk on the hard and unforgiving earth of the *sensus litteralis*. The masters of the sacred page were not of the same mind. Christians had been wandering in the clouds for about a thousand years—from Origen to Anselm—and times were changing. Ralph of Flaix and Bernard of Clairvaux had no doubt that they were changing for the worse. John of Forde was clearly of the same opinion.

The early scholastic commentaries represent the triumph of literal exegesis, a triumph which was to reach its culmination in the canonical statement of Aquinas that the literal sense of scripture was all that the writer intended and that any other interpretation or argument must proceed from this sense alone.[86] The commentary of John of Forde was one of the last attempts at maintaining a tradition which was essentially out of date, and I do not think that John was unaware of this. He suggests in his prologue that some might find his work dull or tasteless (*insipidus*), but he exhorts them at least to try it, and see whether the fault is theirs or that of the work itself.[87] He knows, too, that others will find it too long,[88] but explains that he deliberately avoided brevity on the grounds that simpler minds find it less impressive and because brevity *eximias sententias non pro sua maiestate euolat sed uerborum inuoluat et frangat angustiis*.[89] By John's day, the scholastic *quaestio*—short, snappy, logical—was becoming the preferred mode of thought, and

demonstrates that Langton was aware of the interpretations of Pseudo-Rashi and David Kimhi, but where Langton found the information is unknown. On Langton's commentaries in general, see G. Lacombe and B. Smalley, 'Studies on the Commentaries of Cardinal Stephen Langton, I-II,' *Archives d'histoire doctrinale et littéraire du moyen âge 5* (1930) 5–220. Despite its age this is still essential reading.

86. See B. Smalley, 'William of Auvergne, John of La Rochelle and Saint Thomas Aquinas on the Old Law,' in *Studies*, 164–165 (originally published in *Saint Thomas Aquinas 1274–1974* [Toronto, 1974] 1:10–71).

87. John of Forde, Cant Serm. prolog. 4; CCCM 35, 1.117–119 (CF 29:72).

88. *Ibid.*, 6; p. 36, 145–147 (CF 29:73–74).

89. *Ibid.*, 149–150 (74).

lectio divina itself was being transformed into a more intellectual and scholarly exercise.[90] John has little time for this. He sees himself as following in the footsteps of Bernard[91] and I think we may see his commentary as being in some ways similar to that of Ralph of Flaix. Ralph's long exposition was intended to reassert the value and practice of allegorical exegesis against jewish literalism and jewish argument; the equally long commentary of John was intended to reassert the same thing against the scholastic heirs of the literal movement.

John's vehement denunciation of 'jewish' exegesis, therefore, is not just an attack upon a way of interpretation which had become common and widespread in the twelfth century, but an attack on a way of interpreting scripture which, in his view, was arid, vain, and useless. There is no sound reason for believing that the Cistercians were any more attracted by the methods of scholastic interpretation than anyone else, but neither is there any reason to suppose that they were not equally affected.[92] The works of Peter the Chanter, Peter Comestor, and Stephen Langton were to be found everywhere and were everywhere studied and appreciated,[93] and the voice of John was a voice crying in the wilderness. Ralph of Flaix's commentary, composed half a century earlier, had immense success;

90. See Smalley, *Study*, 281–283 and *idem*, 'Some Thirteenth-Century Commentaries on the Sapiential Books,' *Dominican Studies* 2 (1949) 324.

91. Cant Serm. prolog. 4; 35, 99–108 (CF 29:71–72).

92. I have observed elsewhere that cistercian scholasticism still remains, regrettably, a field almost wholly unexplored: see Bell, 'A Cistercian at Oxford,' 70, n.6.

93. One need only glance at the manuscripts recorded in Stegmüller to see that this is indeed the case. In England, commentaries by Peter the Chanter were at Quarr and Buildwas, and his *Verbum abbreviatum* at Byland, Meaux, and possibly Swineshead. Copies of Comestor's *Historia scholastica* were at Byland, Flaxley, Fountains, Meaux, Swine, and Whalley. Various commentaries by Langton were at Beaulieu, Byland, Coggeshall, Forde, Garendon, Kirkstead, Meaux, Rievaulx, Stratford Langthorne, Valle Crucis, and possibly Croxden. See David N. Bell, *An Index of Authors and Works in Cistercian Libraries in Great Britain*, Cistercian Studies 130 (Kalamazoo, 1992) 112, 113, 136–137.

John's survives in a single manuscript[94] and, so far as I am aware, is reported from only two libraries: Beaulieu and Forde.[95] It is certainly not listed in any other english library catalogue and I have never seen it recorded elsewhere.

Before I conclude this study, however, it might be prudent to consider a possible objection to the thesis presented here. It concerns the commentary on the Song of Songs of Alexander Nequam [Neckham], a commentary which was composed at about the same time as John's and which, like John's, is almost entirely allegorical.[96] It is also equally long (if not longer). Yet there are seven surviving manuscripts and records of a dozen more at other places.[97] Why did Nequam's commentary succeed when John's failed? We must remember four things. Firstly, by the time he produced his commentary, Nequam's name and work (especially his wildly successful *Corrogationes Promethei*) were far better known than those of John of Forde, and writings by authors of established reputation were (and are) far more likely to be purchased and copied than those of comparative obscurities. Secondly, unlike John, Nequam does, in fact, cater to the temper of the times. He appeals to the *hebraica veritas*, and he reports that he has both listened to the expositions of the Jews and has consulted with them.[98] Thirdly, in his use of allegory, Nequam acknowledges that the literal sense remains fundamental and, as Hunt has pointed out, 'in the monastic commentaries his special concern is with tropology',[99] i.e. with that 'biblisch-moralisch' interpretation of the text which we see so clearly in the work of Langton. And finally, it is not really true to say that Nequam's commentary 'succeeded'. There certainly seem to have

94. Oxford, Balliol College, ms 24. See also J. Bale, ed. R. L. Poole and M. Bateson, *Index Britanniae Scriptorum* (Oxford, 1902) 202.

95. See D. N. Bell, 'Lists and Records of Books in English Cistercian Libraries,' *Analecta Cisterciensia* 43 (1987) 184, 194.

96. See the paper by Christopher Holdsworth for a comparison of the two works, pp. 153 to 174 below.

97. See R. W. Hunt, ed. M. Gibson, *The Schools and the Cloister: The Life and Writings of Alexander Nequam (1157–1217)* (Oxford, 1984) 137.

98. See *ibid.*, 108–110.

99. See *ibid.*, 97.

been more copies in various libraries than was the case with John's exposition, but when compared with the distribution of the works of Langton, Comestor, and Peter the Chanter, the numbers are still very few. Furthermore, we have hardly any evidence that anyone ever bothered to read it or use it,[100] and it seems to me that far from disproving the thesis presented in this present study, the case of Nequam's commentary reinforces it. Despite the fact that it was more in touch with the times, it was still too much out of fashion to succeed. Long, prolix, diffuse and allegorical commentaries had no real future.

That the times change and we change with them is undoubtedly true. Some, myself included, would regard this with boundless optimism; John of Forde would simply have found it depressing. His commentary on the Song of Songs may be seen as a reaction against a whole new way of thinking and interpretation, as a last valiant but unsuccessful attempt to return to better and, in his view, richer times. But when he died in 1214 he was buried *sine magna pompa*,[101] a man out of his time. With his death his works, too, lapsed into obscurity and it is only now, some eight hundred years later, that Cistercian Publications has resurrected them and presented them, in english translation, to an infinitely more appreciative audience than ever existed in John's lifetime.

100. See *ibid.*, 122, 124.
101. J. Leland, ed. A. Hall, *Commentarii de Scriptoribus Britannicis* (Oxford, 1709) 231.

Two Commentators on the Song of Songs:
John of Forde and Alexander Nequam

VERY RIGHTLY many of the papers in this volume concentrate upon John of Forde's longest work, his commentary upon the last part of the Song of Songs, written, like Saint Bernard's, in sermon form.[1] For a modern reader it is not easy to read, just because it is so long and seems to stand very much at the end of a long tradition of interpretation both in his own Order and in the monastic world as a whole. Another aspect of it emerges from a reading of the still unedited, and so rarely read, commentary by John's exact contemporary, the augustinian canon, Alexander Nequam, to which David Bell alludes briefly in his study of John's attitude to jewish interpretations of the Bible.[2] It is my hope that a comparison of the two works may cast more light on that issue, and on other characteristics of each writer, as well as raising the possibility that the two men may have known each other's work.

Nequam was an augustinian canon when he wrote on the Song, and a good deal more is known about his life before he joined the community at Cirencester around 1197, than we know of John before he went to Forde.[3] He was born in Saint Albans in 1157 to

---

1. This paper owes an enormous amount to the eagle eye and erudition of my colleague as editor, Hilary Costello.

2. See pages 150–151 above.

3. R. W. Hunt, ed. and revised by Margaret Gibson, *The Schools and the Cloister: The Life and Writings of Alexander Nequam (1157–1217)* (Oxford, 1984) 1–13 for the account which follows.

a mother with the unusual name of Hodierna. There is a tradition that she acted as wet-nurse to the future Richard I, born the same night as Alexander, a tradition given plausibility by the fact that the king provided her with a pension. Alexander was in Paris between about 1175 and 1182, studying at the school on the Petit Pont of which Adam the logician had been the most famous teacher— though he was long dead by 1175, and had probably died soon after Alexander's birth. There he pursued the liberal arts and theology, canon and civil law, as well as medicine. He received, in fact, a training in all the main studies of the schools, though exactly how far he went in any of them is hard to say. On returning to England he became a teacher himself at Dunstable and Saint Albans, in schools under the general oversight of the great monastery of that name. By 1190 he was teaching at Oxford, where no other teacher at that time is known to us by name,[4] and where he lectured on various parts of the Bible. After not very many years there, at some point between 1197 and 1202, he entered religious life at the royal foundation of Cirencester, having undergone some form of conversion experience. Little is known about the internal life of that community that would enable us to know why it attracted Alexander; we know of no group of writers there like that which John found at Forde. But we can be fairly sure that he found a community congenial to writers, since, as Richard Hunt demonstrated many years ago, the english augustinian canons had many writers among their number (though he confessed himself at a loss to suggest reasons for this situation).[5] Like John, Alexander became head of his community, in 1213, the year before John died, and his life ended four years later, early in 1217.

Alexander's career, then, covers very much the same years as John's, and it is at least highly likely that they met at the royal

4. R. W. Southern, 'Master Vacarius and the Beginning of an English Academic Tradition,' in *Medieval learning and Literature, Essays presented to Richard William Hunt*, ed. J. J. G. Alexander and M. T. Gibson (Oxford, 1976) 270.

5. R. W. Hunt, 'English Learning in the late Twelfth Century', in *Essays in Medieval History*, ed. R. W. Southern (London, 1968) 106–128, esp. 120 (reprinted from *Transactions of the Royal Historical Society*, 4th Ser. 19 [1936] 19–42).

court or at gatherings of churchmen, although there is no record that they did.[6] Whereas John's commentary seems to have taken its present shape around 1210, Alexander's was certainly finished before he became abbot of Cirencester, i.e. between 1197/1202 and 1213, though the fact that it contains no reference to the difficult days of the Interdict (of which John does write[7]), may suggest that it was finished by 1208, when the crisis began. I doubt whether we can establish that one of them wrote before the other, so any similarities between the two commentaries may be the result of either writer influencing the other. We should note here, too, that whereas, as far as we know, John's set of one hundred twenty sermons on the Song was his only major writing of the first decade of the thirteenth century, Alexander wrote at least ten substantial works in the fifteen years between his entry to Cirencester and his election as abbot.[8]

His commentary is a very substantial work indeed, occupying over two hundred large folios in most of the seven manuscripts in which it survives.[9] At once we note here a contrast with the narrow circulation of John's works, something increased when one takes into account references to no less than thirteen other manuscripts which once existed. Clearly Alexander's commentary was popular, and marginal notes in the the surviving manuscripts show that it was read and taken seriously well into the fifteenth century.[10] No modern scholar, as far as I know, has yet attempted to discuss it at any length, or to produce a critical edition, which would be a formidable task. Riedlinger, in 1958, devoted some pages to Nequam in his study of commentaries on the Song of Songs, and edited one chapter of it

6. Richard Hunt made this suggestion to me. For John's career, see my discussion, p. 37 above.

7. Cant Serm 41, pp. 298–304 (3:134–146) and 76, pp. 526–534 (5:168–183). For ease of reference I shall give the volume and page number of Beckett's translation of John, but the translations in this article are my own.

8. Hunt, *Schools and Cloister*, 24–28, 125–126.

9. *Ibid.*, 137.

10. Bell, above p. 151, is sceptical about this, but Hunt's evidence, pp. 120–124, is not insignificant, coming from Europe as well as England.

from one manuscript in the Bodleian.[11] Much earlier in the 1930's Richard Hunt used the commentary in his Oxford doctoral thesis upon Nequam, which stayed in manuscript until Margaret Gibson undertook the self-effacing labour of getting it published in 1984 after Hunt's death.[12] Even there, however, not a lot of space is devoted to the commentary. Hunt it was, however, who directed my attention to Alexander when I was working under his supervision, allowing me with typical generosity to read his own thesis, which in its turn impelled me to read the commentary.

In this paper I want to concentrate upon two areas: the general kind of interpretation of the Song which John and Alexander adopted; and the manner in which they approached the text, in particular the amount of attention which they paid to the literal meaning of the text. And then I should like to draw out some other features of their work.

John, as many other chapters in this book remind us, followed his cistercian predecessors in reading the Song as a dialogue between Christ, the Bridegroom, and the individual soul, the Bride, and much of his energy was spent on this interpretation. But he also drew upon three other traditions of explaining the Bride, seeing her as the Church, as the jewish people (as Sister Elizabeth has reminded us[13]), and as the Virgin Mary. The ecclesiological tradition was very old, going back at least to Hippolytus in the the early third century, and it was popularised for the West by Bede, whose commentary was still very much read in the twelfth century.[14] John did not have to explore the meaning of the Bride at length until he reached verses describing

11. H. Riedlinger, *Die Makellosigkeit der Kirche in den lateinischen Hoheliedkommentaren des Mittelalters*, Beiträge zur Geschichte der Philosophie und Theologie des Mittelalters, 38/3 (Münster, 1958) 320–325, and 325–333 for his edition of Book 1:6.

12. See note 3 above.

13. See pp. 117 to 130 above.

14. A useful recent survey of interpretation of the Song is E. Ann Matter, *The Voice of My Beloved: The Song of Songs in Western Medieval Christianity* (Philadelphia, 1990). See the article 'Cantique des Cantiques', by various authors, in the *Dictionnaire de Spiritualité*, 2 (Paris, 1953) cols. 86–109. For John and Alexander and Bede, see pp. 167–168 below.

her with *Pulchra es anima mea* (Sg 6:3). By which point he had written forty-six sermons already, but in these the equations Bride equals individual soul and the Church occur in shorter passages.[15] His first extensive use of the ecclesiological interpretation comes with *Capilli tui sicut grex caprarum* [Sg 6:4] (which he took to stand for the appearance of piety assumed by some members of the Church) and he went on to relate it to the individual soul.[16] From that point on nearly every verse received both an ecclesiogical and individual exposition.

The interpretation of the Bride as the Synagogue, standing for the jewish people, was in some sense a continuation of the jewish interpretation out of which the christian reading Bride equals Church had grown. Certainly from at least Bede's time onwards it was normal to bring the Jews into the Song, and the five places where John does this are all places where earlier commentaries had done so.[17] But his introduction of the reading Bride equals Virgin Mary, represented some deviation from cistercian tradition, as well as from Bede, the *Glossa Ordinaria*, and from Ralph of Laon.[18] By the time John wrote, as is well known, the mariological interpretation had been applied to the whole of the Song by Rupert of Deutz, and by Honorius Augustodunensis, writing in the first two decades of the twelfth century, but how well-known their works were in England

15. Cant Serm XLVII, pp. 332–338 (4:2–15). The first equation Bride = soul is Prol. 3, p. 34 (1:69); the first clear Bride = Church at V. 1, p. 62 (1:126–127). The next sermon also deals with the church, in an explanation not of words in the Song, but of Ezk 36, 37; VI, pp. 65–72 (1:133–145).

16. Cant Serm XLVIIII, pp. 345–353 (4:29–43).

17. Cant Serm LXII (on Sg 6:12) pp. 435–441 (5:1–13); LXIV (Sg 7:1) pp. 447–452 (5:24–35); LXVI (Sg 7:1) pp. 460–465 (5:50–61); XCV (Sg 8:1–2) pp. 642–649 (6:149–163); CII. 10 (Sg 8:5) p. 696 (7:26–28). Compare John with Ralph of Laon, who wrote up his uncle Anselm's teaching: PL 162:1219 (3 times), 1223, 1224. For his work see J. Leclercq, 'Le commentaire du Cantique des Cantiques attribué à Anselme de Laon', *Recherches de Théologie Ancienne et Mediévale* 16 (1949) 29–39.

18. Cant Serm LIX.2–3, 5 (Sg 6:10) pp. 416–417, 418 (4:171–175); LXX (Sg 7:2) pp. 489–494 (5:96–106); LXXIII (Sg 7:4, 'collum tuum') pp. 506–513 (5:130–143); LXXV (Sg 7:4, 'oculi tui') pp. 519–526 (5:155–167). Cf. Bede, *In Cantica Canticorum*, PL 91:1065–1236; *Glossa Ordinaria*, PL 113:1125–1168; Ralph, PL 162:1187–1228.

158

is still an open question. Rupert, according to John Van Engen, was 'almost completely unknown' in England, although over forty manuscripts of his commentary survive, mainly from the Empire.[19] The mariological *Sigillum* of Honorius, on the other hand, survives in five twelfth-century manuscripts, three of them from Worcester, and one each from Evesham and Malmesbury.[20] But, according to the splendid new studies by David Bell, no house of english Cistercians, nor indeed any Gilbertines or Premonstratensians, seem to have had commentaries on the Song by either Rupert or Honorius.[21] This certainly helps to explain why when, in the late twelfth century, another augustinian, William of Newburgh, best known as a historian, tried his hand at interpreting the whole Song in terms of the Virgin, he thought that he was a pioneer.[22]

But whether Rupert and Honorius were known to John, or indeed to Alexander, the liturgical celebrations of the feasts of the Virgin, with their use of passages from the Song, were making the

19. John H. Van Engen, *Rupert of Deutz* (Berkeley, Los Angeles, London, 1983) p. 5.

20. Valerie I. J. Flint, 'The Commentaries of Honorius Augustodunensis on the Song of Songs', *Revue Bénédictine* 84 (1974) p. 197, mentions the english manuscripts of his mariological *Sigillum*, which are listed in her 'The Place and Purpose of the Works of Honorius Augustodunensis', *Rev Bén* 87 (1977) 125–126. The *Sigillum* text is found in PL 172:495–518; an english translation is now available by Amelia Carr, *The Seal of the Blessed Mary by Honorius of Autun (Honorius Augustodunensis)*, Peregrina Translation Series 18 (Toronto, Peregrina Press n.d.). I am grateful to Dr E. Rozanne Elder for drawing my attention to this.

21. David N. Bell, *An Index of Authors and Works in Cistercian Libraries in Great Britain*, CS 130 (Kalamazoo, 1992), and his *The Libraries of the Cistercians, Gilbertines and Premonstratensians*, Corpus of British Medieval Library Catalogues, 3 (London, 1992). The *Registrum Anglie de Libris Doctorum et Auctorum Veterum*, ed. R. A. B. Mynors, Richard H. Rouse, Mary A. Rouse (Corpus, 2, London, 1991), does not contain the commentaries either.

22. *William of Newburgh's Explanatio Sacri Epithalamii in Matrem Sponsi*, ed. John C. Gorman, Spicilegium Friburgense 6 (Fribourg, 1960) p. 21, drawing attention to William's own words at p. 71 in his preface to Roger of Byland.

interpretation Bride equals Mary very widely known indeed.[23] It is, therefore, not surprising that John says that his audience expected him to apply certain verses of the Song to the Virgin. Writing of the verse 'Thy eyes are like the pools in Esebon, which are in the gate of the daughter of the people' [Sg 7:4], for example, he commented,

> If I defrauded the Mother of the Lord of her praise in this marriage-song, especially when her praise shines out not a little from this present image, I would fear lest my own mouth should condemn me.[24]

Nevertheless, his use of the Marian approach to the text was restrained in comparison with Alexander's, to which we now turn.

For Alexander the Song was above all to be read as a passionate exchange between Christ and the Virgin Mary. In his first book, which forms an extended prologue to the work, he writes of her conception, birth, life, marriage, and of the annunciation, the whole forming a kind of spiritualised *Vita,* with its climax in the Incarnation.[25] At the start of Book Two he takes, at last, the opening phrase of the Song, *Osculetur me osculo oris sui.* But just where one might think that he would get down to the text seriatim, he spends no less than six chapters exploring a number of general questions, for example, why the Song is called an epithalamium, and why some texts call it the Song of Songs, and some the Songs of Songs.[26] Here, in fact, many of the themes discussed in other prefaces to a commentary appear, but this must be one of the most

---

23. The emergence of the mariological tradition is well discussed by Matter (note 14 above) pp. 151–177; cf. Ann W. Astell, *The Song of Songs in the Middle Ages* (Ithaca and London, 1990) pp. 42–50, 60–72.

24. Cant Serm LXXV.1, p. 520 (5:155).

25. Book 1:1–17, British Library, Royal ms 4 D XI (from which all other quotations come), fos. 3b-44va. A thorough comparison between Nequam and his predecessors may well be worth making. The pattern of this first book folows that set by Rupert (for which see Astell, p. 61) on a much vaster scale.

26. Royal ms, fos. 3a-9a.

160

extended discussions of its kind.[27] It includes an interesting passage in which he explains the different levels of meaning to be found in the text.

The first meaning he discerns in the Song is the marriage of Christ with the Church, which he calls the allegorical meaning, but he said that because many other authors had dealt with it extensively, he did not intend to do so himself, except occasionally. At a second level the Song is about the marriage of the Virgin and Christ which was found partly through allegory, partly through anagogy. 'To explain this', he added, 'was the purpose of his work so long as the Virgin herself' was willing to be his guide, and it was to her hands that he offered the work 'prostrate before the feet of her goodness.' Lastly, the Song concerned the marriage of God and the faithful soul, discovered by tropology, which he said he would also use.[28] This programme he did in fact follow fairly consistently through the whole of his commentary, but although every verse receives a mariological meaning, not every verse is expounded in terms of the church or of the individual soul, but most are.

Alexander was then, like John, writing a commentary at a number of levels, but unlike John he used all the traditional terms for these levels. At one point he described the Bible as being like a cellar stocked with four sorts of barrel which are history, allegory, tropology, and anagogy. The first is fit for the simple, inviting them to

27. A. J. Minnis, *Medieval Theory of Authorship* (2nd. ed. Aldershot, 1988) pp. 40–72.
28. Book 2:5, Royal ms f.47 va 'Non est autem intentionis nostre propositum epithalamium amoris exponere de Christo et ecclesia, quia multa nobilia opera tam eleganter quam diligenter super hoc edita sunt . . . Quandoque tamen allegorice expositioni opus nostrum deseruiet . . . Beata igitur Uirgo ratione carnis assumpte a Verbo, sponsa est . . . Nobilissimo ergo matrimonio quod in coniunctione deitatis et humane nature consistit, deseruit canticum quod in parte/f.47vb anagogicum, ex parte allegoricum est. Hoc canticum explanare propositum est negotii nostri, dum modo Beata Virgo dux operis nostri esse dignetur, cuius manibus hoc opus offero, prouolutus ad pedes benegnitatis ipsius. Est item dulce matrimonium inter Deum et animam fidelem, sed et ipsum reperiet diligens lector in hoc dulcissimo opere Salomonis. Huic matrimonio competit canticum tropologice dulcedinis cui deseruire plerumque studebimus.'

love God; the second conveys the clarification of faith, whereas the third concerns the forming of behaviour; anagogy, the last, contains in the subtlest way, an understanding of heavenly things.[29] The same image of the cellar is expounded rather differently in another place with the historical meaning coming first, but then follows the moral meaning, with allegory and anagogy completing the quartet.[30] The categorisation of levels, indeed, varies, so that the historical is called the literal sense, or the tropological called moral, or the three meanings which do not arise immediately from the text are occasionally lumped together as the spiritual sense.

Such terminology did not come to John's mind, although it must have been familiar to him from books he had read, and he shows quite clearly that he understood that a text contained various levels of meaning within it. It is instructive to see, for example, how he used the idea of Scripture as a wine-cellar, which he, like Alexander, took from Song 2.4, *Introduxit me rex in cellam vinariam, et ordinavit in me caritatem.*

> The words of wisdom are rich in senses, like a rich man's
> wine-cellar . . . [he wrote]. There is softer wine and stronger

29. Book 3:15 Royal ms f.86a: 'Cella etiam uinaria sacra scriptura dici solet. In hac cella sunt quatuor genera doliorum, que sunt historia, allegoria, tropologia et anagoge. In primo dolio continetur uinum quo simplices potandi sunt. Factis enim antiquorum et exemplis, ad honestatis amorem inuitandi sunt. Allegoria continet elucidationem fidei. Tropologia se debet morum compositio. In quarto dolio continetur uinum subtilissime comprehensionis supra celestium.' This may be compared with Book 2:2: likening the meanings to various foods, Royal ms, f. 46va: 'Quibusdam mel tropologice dulcedinis: aliis buturum suauitatis allegorice: non nullis oues simplicitatis litteralis intelligentie: aliquibus pingues uitulos anagogice subtilitatis apponimus.' See Hunt, *Schools and Cloister*, pp. 95–97, for other examples of Alexander's use of the four senses.
30. Royal ms, f.58b: 'In cellarium uero misteriorum eloquii diuini inducta sponsa, nec est contenta simplici et communi uino historalis intelligentie, licet placidi saporis sit; aut uino moralis intellectus et si suauissimum saporis deliciis commendabile sit; aut uino iocundissimi saporis quo gloriatur allegoria, sed introductam se fatetur in penitiores partes cellarii iam dicti, ubi subtilissimo uino intelligentie anagogice exhilaratam esse se innuit.'

wine for those more eminent in understanding and more capable of drinking. There is the wine which he mixes for his friends, that which he offers to his dearest friends, that which he presses for the family, and that which he measures out for those of weaker capacity.[31]

Here John divides his wines out, not according to the scheme of the four senses, but according to a scale which measures ability to accept. Elsewhere he expressed a similar concept of biblical meanings when he called the Bible a wood which had its thickets, where dense mysteries could be found (the wood image was one used by Gregory the Great), and both he and Alexander took up another well-worn image when they called the Bible a mirror.[32] Nequam developed this image particularly well, pointing out how no one could see himself unless he looked in a mirror, and how the image there altered as one held the mirror near to, or away from, oneself.[33] Where John and Alexander differed enormously was in the kind of attention which they paid to the literal meaning of the text.

For John this was a stage preparatory to the real stuff of his search for meaning: 'For we must first consider the form of this praise, even if rather superficially, so that once her holy clothing has been stripped off, the very face of truth may emerge more splendidly.'[34] One ought, according to John, to move quickly to the inner levels.

31. Cant Serm LVII.1, p. 400 (4:138).

32. Cant Serm LXXII.8, p. 505 (5:127); Gregory, *Moralia*, 33.2 (PL 76:669, or better, *CCCM*, 143B:1670); Cant Serm LXXXV.4, p. 583 (6:29). The mirror image was popularised by John of Fécamp and used by many after him; cf. J. Leclercq, *L'Amour des Lettres et le Désir de Dieu* (Paris, 1957) p. 79.

33. Book 2:23, Royal ms, f.66b: 'Per speculum, sacra scriptura intelligitur. Faciem propriam intueri non potes nisi in speculo . . . Sacram scripturam lector inspice sedulus, et statueris contra faciem tuam. In illo [ie. speculo] notabis sordes corporis, in ista [ie. sacra scriptura], immunditias spirituales deprehendes. Admoue speculum materiale propinquius faciei tue, et uicinior tibi uidebitur facies inspecta. Tene speculum remotius, remotior tibi uidebitur facies resultans in speculo. Familiaris tibi sit sacre pagine inspectio, et familiarius teipsum agnosces.'

34. Cant Serm XXV.1, p. 209 (2:147).

It is therefore not surprising to find that he briefly examined the grammar and syntax of the text, but went no further at that level. A typical example comes in his very first full sermon where he draws attention to the actual words which the Bride uses: 'She does not say "I am sick with love, or I am weak with love (*amore egroto vel amore infirmor*), but I languish for love" (*amore langueo*), thus indicating the length of her sickness and the difficulty of her cure.'[35]

Sometimes he deliberately renounced any attempt to look hard at words on the grounds of his lack of expertise; for example, 'If there is indeed a difference between thigh (*femur*) and leg (*crus*), I leave it to those more skilled in Latin to settle. It is no concern of mine, for I have heard both words used indifferently in the Bible.'[36]

Such an attitude would have struck Alexander as cavalier and unscholarly. For him the establishment of the literal meaning was the necessary foundation without which the house of spiritual understanding had no sound basis.[37] To dig such a foundation Alexander used many tools; a comparison of various Latin versions of the Bible, consultation with a rich tradition of christian commentaries on the Song, and, less typically for his age, comparison with the Hebrew text of the Old Testament, and with jewish exegesis.[38] So, for example, he notes that one latin version differs from the Vulgate at the start of the Song reading, *Osculetur me ab osculis oris sui* instead of *Osculetur me osculo oris sui*.[39] Often he draws

35. Cant Serm I.5, pp. 42–43 (1:84).
36. Cant Serm XXXIII.2, p. 256 (3:50).
37. Book 3:12, Royal ms, f.83: 'Sic sic in multis sacre scripturis locis frustra manum consummationis adhibere studebit scribentis diligentia erectioni edificii spiritualis intelligentie, nisi certum subiciat fundamentum sensus litteralis.' One may note in 'sic sic' one of Alexander's favourite rhetorical figures, *anadiplosis*: see Hunt, *Schools and Cloister*, p. 64, and pp. 97–107 for a discussion of his characteristics as a commentator.
38. There is at least one case where he mentions Greek: Book 3:17, Royal ms, f.89a (On Sg 2:9, 'Similis est dilectus meus capree, hinnuloque ceruorum'); 'Caprea igitur ab acumine uisus Grece *dorchas* dicitur.' Hunt, *Schools and Cloister*, p. 108 thought that he only knew the letters of the greek alphabet. This example could, I suppose, have come from a bestiary.
39. Book 2:8, Royal ms, f.49va: 'Attendite quia cum alia translatio dicat, osculetur me ab osculis oris sui, in nostra editione habetur, osculetur me

attention to the Septuagint readings where they seem to him relevant. Quite early in his commentary, for example, he notes a difference between the normal text of Genesis 47:31 and the Septuagint.[40] Here he shows the precision of a scholar quite out of keeping with John's basic approach. He lays hold, too, on a wide range of earlier authors, whom generally he names: Augustine, Jerome, Ambrose and Gregory, as well as Chrysostom and Bede.[41] He also enriched his argument with extracts from ancient poets and philosophers—Ovid, Vergil, and Plato, for example.[42] As is well-known now thanks to the edition and translation, John almost never cites another author, though he refers twice to Augustine, once to Ambrose, and five times to Gregory, as well as once to Anselm among those nearer his own day. In one passage he names all of these together with some of his cistercian predecessors, Bernard, Guerric of Igny, and Gilbert of Hoyland, as well as the great mystical theologian, Richard of Saint Victor, and I think most of us would probably agree that it is these to whom he owed most.[43] But the greatest contrast between John and Alexander is in their attitude to anything to do with Jewish understanding, a matter also explored by David Bell.

---

osculo oris sui. Utriusque editionis auctor est spiritus sanctus, utraque digna veneratione.'

40. Book 1:11, Royal ms, f.21a: 'Vbi enim in Genesi legimus, quo iurante adorauit Israel Deum conversus ad lectuli caput, in translatione lxxta reperitur, et adorauit contra summitatem uirge.' Similar passages are numerous, eg. Book 3:7, Marginal note on f.77vb (on Sg 1:12 'Fasciculus myrrhe dilectus meus mihi; inter ubera mea commorabitur'): 'Alligamentum gutte fraternus meus mihi. Translatio autem lxxa habet, Colligatio gutte, consobritius meus mihi.'

41. Augustine, Jerome, and Chrysostom all on Royal ms f.26a: Ambrose, f.175b-175va; Gregory, f.106a, 126a, 157bv; Bede, f.33va, 135vb (these are merely examples).

42. Royal ms, f.36va (Ovid) 'Tu citius uenias / portus et aura tuis.'; f.34b, (Vergil, 'in bucolicis' marg.) 'Frigidus o pueri fugite hinc, latet anguis in herba.' (ie. = Eclogues, III.93); f.105va 'Uoluptates, inquit, Plato, sunt esca malorum qua quidem infelices homines seducuntur, sicut hamo pisces capiuntur.' (=Cicero, Cato Major de Senectute, 13.149). These identifications I owe to Hilary Costello. Cf. Hunt, Schools and Cloister, pp. 43–53, for Alexander's use and knowledge of the classics.

43. Cant Serm XXIV.2, p. 203 (2:135). See also the Index Sanctorum Patrum and Index Nominum in Cant Serm, pp. 872–877, 878–881.

Just about forty years ago Raphael Loewe published an important paper upon Alexander's knowledge of Hebrew, which has not, as far as I know, been superseded by more recent work. He argued that Alexander 'evinces quite a considerable familiarity with jewish exegesis and lore, and was interested in jewish opinion and practice'. Such familiarity and interest, as well as what Loewe called an 'elementary knowledge of Hebrew' did not put Alexander as an hebraist on the same level as Herbert of Bosham, perhaps the most remarkable christian hebraist of his generation, but it does give his commentary a character all its own.[44] Again and again he noted differences between the hebrew text and that of various christian versions of the Old Testament, and at numerous points refers to a learned Jew *'litterator Hebreus'*, someone who still remains to be identified (in other works he names Gamaliel, whom Hunt identifies with the Talmud).[45] The two extracts which follow are examples of the kind of comments which occur again and again. Where he deals with Song 1:2, *Oleum effusum nomen tuum*, he writes 'Those who are learned in the idiom of the hebrew language, assert that in Hebrew it reads "*Oleum effundens nomen tuum*' ".[46] Explaining Song 2:14, *Surge, amica mea, speciosa mea, et veni*, Alexander states 'The jewish teacher, however, punctuates thus "Rise up my friend and my bride, and come' ".[47] On one occasion he stigmatised the jewish reading of a verse as 'laughable', but generally treated it with respect.[48] John,

44. R. Loewe, 'Alexander Neckham's Knowledge of Hebrew", *Mediaeval and Renaissance Studies* 4 (1958) pp. 17–34.

45. See Hunt, *Schools and Cloister*, pp. 108–110.

46. Book 2:13, Royal ms, f. 54va: 'Litteratores tamen quidam in idiomate sermonis Hebrei, asserunt in Hebreo contineri oleum effundens nomen tuum.'

47. Book 3:22, Royal ms, f.94va: 'Litterator tamen hebreus litteram sic distinguit, "Surge amica mea et sponsa mea, et ueni." '

48. Book 5:9, Royal ms, f.149vb-150a. 'Dum pueriles hebreorum expositiones quas loco isti adaptant reduco ad memoriam, nescio utrum risum an dolorem procreare possint lectori maturi pectoris. Risum excitare uidebuntur, dum superficialem quandam expositionem eis que hic propununtur accommodant [ms accomodant], tam friuolam quam comtemptibilem dolorem, eo quod supina et crassa ignorantia obtenebratum est insipiens cor eorum [Rom 1:21].'

as David Bell shows, would have disapproved of this side of Alexander's work, since he condemned the jewish reading of Scripture as 'wild and ridiculous'. I will not, therefore, discuss John's attitude to this issue, but merely note how different it was to Alexander's.

A thorough discussion of the two commentaries would take me far beyond the bounds of a short paper, but I want to highlight briefly five points. Firstly, both Alexander and John frequently refer to interpretations of the text which they assume will be well known to their readers. Nequam calls them the 'common reading' and sometimes the marginal or interlinear gloss,[49] whereas John writes more vaguely of the reading of 'many wise men'.[50] In Nequam's case such readings do not correspond with those found in the, admittedly very inadequate, edition of the *Glossa Ordinaria* in the *Patrologia Latina*, but Hunt was able to find similar references in his *Gloss on the Psalter* in manuscripts of the *Glossa*. With John, on the other hand, such references can be found in the same edition, and, incidentally, in other commentaries which may have been drawn on by the *Glossa*. But neither of them felt inhibited from moving on from the main line tradition to their own track. John, for example, began his exposition of 'My beloved is white and ruddy' with the Gloss's view that whiteness stood for Christ's innocence, and redness for his suffering.[51] But he then developed these ideas with

49. Eg. Book 5:13, Royal ms, f.158b 'Interlinearis enim deseruiens misterio predicti transitus Geneseos dicit.': *Ibid*, f.158va 'Alie quidem expositiones illi transitui adhibentur, sed hec profertur aliis in marginali.'; Book 6:3, f.168a: 'Secundum communem expositionem . . .' and f.168va: 'Secundum communem lectionem . . . .' Cf Hunt's discussion, pp. 97–102. There is clearly need for further work in this area.

50. Cant Serm LXXIX.1, p. 547 (5:209); cf. Glossa Ordinaria, PL 113:1162. The same interpretation occurs in Bede, Ralph of Laon and Robert of Tombelaine; PL 91:1193; 162:1220; 79:535. As yet no one, I think, has compared John's interpretations with those of Bernard, whom he so much admired. Cf. Cant Serm Prologus 4, p. 35 (1:72): 'Habeat sibi uir excellentissimus, cuius laus est in epithalamio, priuilegium gloriae suae, ut quae singulariter per spiritum caritatis expertus est, ceteris fragantius per spiritum sapientiae eructare meruerit.'

51. Cant Serm III–X, pp. 48–100 (1:97–200); Glossa, PL 91:1161 'Et bene primo candidus, deinde rubicundus, quia primo sanctus uenit in mundum, et postmodum sua passione cruentus exiuit de mundo.'

incredible fulness, over eight sermons. Parts of his discussion here seem to me to be unparalleled in other writers, although I have only consulted a selection: Bede, the *Glossa*, a commentary written at Laon, Robert of Tombelaine, Rupert of Deutz and Alexander.[52] His fulness, which established his main exegetical principles, may have been a deliberate imitation of Benard's first eight sermons which did the same by concentrating on one verse.[53]

Secondly, both John and Alexander often went back to Bede. Although John never actually named him, his dependence may be deduced from verbal similarities. One may cite, for example, a passage early on in the commentary:

'What sort of beloved is your beloved?' That is to say, 'Which part of him is loved by you?' For truly he has that majesty for which he ought properly to be feared, and he has that benevolence for which he deserves to be loved.[54]

This contains a stirking similarity with Bede on the same passage:

'Come tell me, what sort of beloved is your beloved?' that is to say, which part of him ought to be loved rather than feared?[55]

The phrase *ex ea parte* is not of course, long, but the likelihood that John took it from Bede seems high when one realises that it is not used by any other commentator whom I have consulted, except, perhaps, one associated with Stephen Langton.[56] As for

---

52. For the first four, see note 50 above. Rupert's *Commentarius in Cantica Canticorum* in PL 168:839–962, or better, CCCM 26 (Turnholt, 1974).

53. I owe this suggestion to Hilary Costello.

54. 'Qualis est dilectus tuus ex dilecto? Id est, ex ea parte qua, a te diligitur. Habet namque maiestas illa quod sive debeat timeri; habet benignitas illla quod mereatur amari.' Cant Serm II.3, p. 47 (1:94).

55. 'Dic ergo, age, *qualis est dilectus tuus ex dilecto*? Hoc est, ex ea parte qua diligi debeat potius quam timeri.' PL 91:1161.

56. Oxford, Bodleian Library, ms Bodley 528, f.71v. 'Vel enim dilectus ex dilecto, Christus ex ea parte qua diligendus est, non ex ea qua timendus.'

Nequam, thanks to his marginal notes, it is quite clear that he used Bede extensively, just as he did in his commentary on Proverbs. Here, for example, commenting on Song 5:1 *Veniat dilectus meus in hortum suum, et comedat fructum pomorum suorum*, the issue of whether the risen Christ had really eaten, as Peter claimed (Acts 10:41), was raised in his mind. To solve this Nequam turned to Bede:

> Bede says on this passage 'Here Peter explains something about which the Gospel is silent, that he ate with Christ after the resurrection: unless we believe that this was indicated where he said, "I will not drink from henceforth of the fruit of the vine until the Kingdom of God shall come" ' [Lk 22:18], that is after the resurrection.

When one turns to Bede's works, it emerges that Alexander was using his commentary not on the Song, nor on Acts, but on Luke, and that he was not citing him directly but summarising him.[57] Both works, therefore, seem to me to bear interesting testimony to the continuing influence of the Northumbrian nearly five hundred years after his death.

Thirdly, I have noticed two places where John and Alexander use an interpretation which I have been unable to find elsewhere, including in Saint Bernard's work on the Song. These are worth a closer look. The first is the link that they both make between Song 6.4, *Averte oculos tuos a me*, with Jesus's words to the disciples in John 16.7: *Ego veritatem dico vobis, expedit vobis ut ego vadam. Nisi enim abiero, Paraclitus non veniet ad vos*. From this injunction they each deduce the meaning that if Christ had not removed himself from the carnal eyes of the disciples, they would not have been

---

57. Book 5:2, Royal ms f.135vb: 'Super quem locum dicit Beda; Hic exponit Petrus, quod in euangelio tacetur, post resurrectionem se bibisse cum Christo, nisi illic credamus indicatum ubi ait, "Non bibam amodo uobiscum genimine uitis antequam bibam illud uobiscum in regno patris mei", id est post resurrectionem.' Cf. Bede, *In Luce Euangelium Expositio*, Book VI (PL 92:596, or better, CCCM 120:377). For Alexander's lengthy citations of Bede in other works, Hunt, *Schools and Cloister*, p. 105.

able to see spiritually. Their actual words, however, do not seem to imitate each other.[58] The other similarity occurs towards the end of their commentaries where they tackle the final verse of the Song, *Fuge, dilecte mi*, and liken this last outburst of the Bride with Peter's desperate appeal to Jesus *Exi a me quia homo peccator sum, domine* [Lk 5:8].[59] Both these conjunctions are so striking that they raise the question whether they were both drawing on some common source, one which I have so far failed to identify, or whether they influenced each other.

My fourth point arises from the by now obvious observation that both Alexander and John, in their different ways were learned men. Yet now I want to ask, how did they regard the knowledge which could be obtained in the world with that which could be found in the cloister? Both of them reckoned it as much less significant, a view hardly surprising in John's case since, as far as we can see now, he had been very much formed in the cloister, but perhaps more unusual for someone like Alexander, a recruit to the religious life in his forties.[60] In a striking passage he lamented the preference he

58. Cant Serm XLVIII.5–6, pp. 341–342 (4:20–22); Alexander, Book 5:12, Royal ms, f.156b: 'In oculis item qui nuntii sunt amoris interioris, teneritudo dilectionis exprimitur. Carnalis igitur amor qui in discipulis Domini erat dum corporali eius presentia fruebantur, commutandus erat in spiritualem amorem. Subtrahenda itaque erat corporali Domini presentia oculis teneri amoris, ut aduentu Spiritus Sancti corda amantium igne divino accenderentur in amorem spiritualem, et ad robur fortitudinis perseuerantis consolidarentur. Expedit inquit Dominus discipulis ut ego uadam. Si enim non abiero, paraclitus/f.156va non ueniet ad uos.'.

59. Cant Serm CXX.7, p. 810 (7:247); Alexander, Book 6:23, Royal ms, f.203a: 'Adde quod dum anima hinc maiestatis dignitatem inde meritorum propriorum non solum insufficientiam sed indignitatem attendit, dicere potest cum Petro, "Recede a me domine, quia homo peccator sum.' " Alexander's 'Recede' for 'Exi' may suggest that he was using a different version of Peter's words, or, as Hilary Costello has suggested to me, that he had confused the Gospel pericope with others in which God, or a person, is repulsed by someone guilty of sinfulness where *recede* is used; i.e., Gen 13:9, Ex 10:28, 4 K 18:14.

60. For John and the monastery as a school of love, see C. J. Holdsworth, 'John of Ford and English cistercian writing 1167–1214', *Transactions of the Royal Historical Society*, 5th Ser. 11 (1961) 134–136.

found among some religious for what he had come to feel were lower matters, which they should have left behind:

> Just as Lot's wife was bewitched into a pillar of salt, so it seems to me have men clothed in religious habits been changed, who prefer the love of secular letters to the spiritual delights of the heavenly page [i.e. Scripture]. They linger among other studies, the rules of grammar, particularly the common readings of dialectic, the aphorisms of rhetoric, the axioms of arithmetic, music, the theorems of geometry, the rules of astronomy, the laws of Justinian, the aphorisms of Hippocrates, but, alas, Holy Scripture is not thought worthy to be admitted within their thresholds.[61]

Elsewhere he denounced the preference of many religious for hearing about the marriage of Mercury and Philosophy (that is to say, the book of Martianus Capella on the Liberal Arts), rather than the Song on the marriage of Christ and the Church. They preferred to hear the name of Hymen rather than the sweet name of Jesus.[62] John, clearly, also felt depressed by his monks' choice of conversation, lamenting that they preferred to gossip about 'the progeny of bulls, ploughs . . . and the yields of fields' rather than 'Jesus and the Songs of Syon'.[63] Nonetheless, Alexander, like so many before him believed

61. Book 6:5, Royal ms, f.169va: 'Cum uxore Loth in statuam salis infatuati, mutari michi uidentur uiri religionis habitu decorati qui secularium litterarum amorem spiritualibus preferunt deliciis pagine celestis. Detineant aliorum studium regule grammatice, maxime dialectice communes loci, rethorice aporismata, arismetice anxiomata, musice, geometrie theoremata, canones astronomie, regule iuris Iustiniani, Ypocratis aphorismi, sed utinam ne intra penates suos admittere dignetur sacra scriptura.'

62. Alexander, Book 2:10, Royal ms, f.51vb: 'Quid est ergo uiri fratres, quod multi etiam claustrales, pro dolor, libentius et affectuosius audiunt librum compositum de nuptiis Mercurii et Philogie, quam nuptiale carmen [corr. in ms from carnem] editum de nuptiis Christi et ecclesie?' *De nuptiis Philologiae et Mercurii*, ed. A. Dick (Stuttgart: Teubner, 1969, rev. ed.) trans. in W. H. Stahl, R. Johnson and E. L. Burge, *Martianus Capella and the Seven Liberal Arts* (New York and London: Columbia University Press, 1977).

63. Cant Serm CXV.7, p. 778 (7:185–186).

that the liberal arts were useful for the study of Scripture. 'The liberal arts rejoiced to be handmaidens of theology', he wrote, going on to ask, as though expecting a negative answer, whether 'the flowers of Quintilian or the colours of Cicero could confer anything upon the beauty of the words of Scripture.'[64]

It is no surprise, therefore, to find that Alexander, unlike some of his confrères, among them Alexander, canon of Canons Ashby, was suspicious of the tendency to apply the techniques of rhetoric to the task of preaching.[65] In one place he stated quite clearly that tricks derived from Quintilian or Cicero should not be used by the preacher, because they would turn what should be something for the good of its hearers into a display of boasting and rare learning.[66] But it is quite clear that he was rejecting something which he knew about. Twice he explains unfinished statements in the text of the Song by saying that they were examples of the rhetorical figure *aposiopesis*, a figure described in *Ad Herennium*, as well, no doubt, as in works written in Alexander's day.[67] In another passage commenting on Song 2:3 *Sicut malus inter ligna siluarum, sic dilectus meus inter filios*, Alexander drew on both the rhetorical figure antonomasia,

64. Alexander, Book 4:20, Royal ms, f.127a: 'Artes liberales se gloriantur ancillas esse theologie. Quid Quintiliani flores, quid Ciceronis colores conferre presumes uenustati sermonis pagine celestis?'

65. For the other Augustinian canon see Hunt, 'English learning', p. 115.

66. Alexander, Book 5:9, Royal ms, f.149vb: 'Perperam interpretari uidentur transitum istum qui eloquia diuina ideo censent dici lilia, quia sermones ad utilitatem proximorum in medium propendos ornandos esse reputant floribus Quintiliani, Ciceronis coloribus depingendois, firmatibus distinctionum decorandos. Sed quid? nonne eloqui Domini eloquia casta sunt [Ps 11:7]? Prostantis est, fucis emendicatis faciem ornare oculos stibio depingere. Caste uero cerussam non mendicant, nec alienum adoptant colorem, fine coli modio deiderant . . . . Uendicat sibi laborem predicantis fauor popularis, dum officium institutum gratia publice utilitatis, transit in officium iactantie et curiositatis.'

67. Alexander, Book 2:23, f.65vb: 'Dulciter igitur commemorans mater dulcedinis filio beneficia collata, utitur aposiopese dicens, "Si igitur ignoras . . . [Sg 1:7].' F. 66 vb; 'Similiter et hic cum dicitur, "Si ignoras te o pulchra inter mulieres" aposiopesis est.'; *Ad Herennium* IV.xxx (Loeb ed. p. 331).

and jewish understanding, besides making what seems like an early reference to oranges in England.

> And so by the excellence of antonomasia the apple is here said to be that most beautiful tree, of whose fruit the sons of Israel were ordered to take with the branches of the palm trees when they dwelt in their shade [Lev 23:40, 42]. But the modern Jews are deceived reckoning the lemon to be the fruit of the most beautiful tree. It is, really, the fruit tree which bears apples of golden colour, so that they are called golden apples, just as the poet said 'I have sent ten golden apples and you will have others when I send them.'

Against these words there is a marginal note in a contemporary hand 'In French language, orange apples.'[68] I think any reading of John shows that he, too, knew some of the tricks and colours recommended by classical rhetoricians (here, again , there is still ample room for a paper on his style), but I do not think that one can find such explicit use of the terms of rhetoric as Alexander's. His learning is, perhaps, less studied, and he followed Bernard in being able to weave his own thoughts according to the pattern available in the words of the Bible.

John and Alexander appear, as a result of this comparison of their commentaries on the Song, to be men of knowledge and

68. Book 3:12, Royal ms, f.83a 'Per excellentiam itaque antonomasie malus hic dicitur arbor illa pulcherrima, cuius fructus sumi precipitur filiis Israel cum palm-/f83b arum spatulis, dum in umbraculis habitant. Falluntur autem Hebrei moderni, existimantes pomum citrinum esse fructum arboris pulcherrime. Est enim arbor ista, malus ferens poma aurei coloris, unde et mala aurea dicuntur secundum quod ait poeta: "Aurea mala decem misi eras altera mittam.'" Marginal note: 'In galliaco ydiomate, pumes orenges.' For antinomasia, *Ad Herennium*, IV, xxxi 42 (p. 335). Hyperbaton and resis occur at f.86b: 'Sed huiuscemodi yperbaton non sustinet scema reseos, et si tam dianeos quam lexeos scema, id sustineat.' Here a series of differently arranged dots above yperbaton, dianeos and lexeos, lead the eye to the marginal note 'Hyperbaton est longa suspensio cum aliquorum interpositione. Resis est ornatus rethoricus, constructionis dialectice.' For hyperbaton cf. *Ad Herennium* IV.xxxii, ed. p. 337. I find the rest hard to follow.

skill, but concerned to explore the text in rather different ways. Nequam's quarrying into its literal meaning would have struck John as dangerously beside the point, since the inner meaning which he sought did not depend upon it, whereas the very letter was for Alexander crucial to anything which might lie within. Yet, both of them, and this is a matter which there is no space to pursue here, were deeply involved in that inner message, the spiritual teaching there.

Differences there certainly were in their approaches, but the two similarities in their interpretation of verses from the Song raise the teasing and unanswerable question which I have already mentioned: did they know one another's work? The likelihood that they had met, at least, seems high, and as we leave them I want to draw attention to a remarkable passage in Alexander's commentary in which he breaks forth in praise of the Cistercians, during the course of expounding Canticles 7:11, *Veni, dilecti mi, egrediamur in agrum, commoremur in villis.*

Often when I turn my attention to this place, the venerable Cistercian Order occurs in my thoughts, who at one time with Isaac go out into the field to work, and at another are happily wrapt in the delights of sweetest contemplation. They dwell in towns, because every one of their dwellings can rightly be called Capernaum, which means the most beautiful town. They sow in tears of devotion which water the land of free will, but they reap in joy. Returning home they return with joy, bearing their sheaves. O worthy order who, because you are fed with the labours of your hands, will be blessed and all will be well with you.[69]

69. Alexander, Book 6:14, Royal ms, f.185a, with marginal note in red 'De cisterciensibus': 'Quotiens ad hunc locum me transfero, meditationibus meis occurrit uenerabilis ordo Cisterciensium, qui nunc cum Ysaac egrediuntur in agrum ad exercitandum, nunc contemplationis dulcissime deliciis feliciter detinentur. Commorantur in uillis, quia quelibeg ipsorum mansio recte dici Capharnaum, id est uilla pulcherrima. Hi seminant in lacrimis deuotionis irrigantibus terram liberi arbitrii, sed in exultatione metent.

His praise continues, building around successive phrases from the next two verse of the Song, and ends,

> You offer to your Beloved new and old apples, because you consecrate to God both the the young fruits of your young men, and the riper fruits of your white-haired men. I glory in having fallen into your praise, because my praise can not attain to the peak of your perfection.[70]

The Cistercians often came in for criticism just as Alexander broke out in this extraordinary paeon. Was he, I wonder, moved by what he had read about, or indeed seen at, the community led during those years by his contemporary John at Forde ? I like to think so.

Uenientes autem uenient cum exultatione, portantes manipulos suos. O commendabilis ordo, qui quia labores manuum tuarum manducabis, beatus es et bene tibi erit.'

70. Royal ms f.185b: 'Omnia poma noua et uetera dilecto uestro seruantis, quia et fructus adolescentie uestre nouellos, et maturos uenerabilis caniciei fructus, Deo dicatis. In laude uestri glorior me succumbere, quia non potest ad culmen uestre perfectionis mea laus attingere.' He bursts into another, but shorter, praise of the Order at Book 6:17; Royal ms f. 192b–192va.

Avril Henry

John of Forde and *The Mirour of Mans Saluacioune*

IN AN ANONYMOUS fifteenth-century Middle English translation that survives in only one manuscript, a brief and abbreviated
marginal reference provides what may be rare, albeit limited, evidence of John of Forde's readership in England during the late
Middle Ages. This discovery is not mine: it was made by my former
colleague and present friend Christopher Holdsworth, whose name
should therefore rightly appear rather at the end than the beginning
of this paper. My sole qualification for presenting this material is the
doubtful one of having been unable to recognise the source referred
to in the marginal reference, with the result that, as so often, I sought
the ever-ready help of our resident St Bernard expert. This paper
describes the context of the reference to John of Forde, but also
raises more questions than I am currently able to answer. Herein lies
whatever interest it may have for specialists in Cistercian studies.

The unique manuscript in which the marginal reference occurs is
The Mirour of Mans Saluacioune,[1] a slavishly literal and occasionally confused translation of the equally anonymous but very well

1. The manuscript is in the private Foyle collection at Beeleigh Abbey,
near Maldon, Essex. The edition, *The Mirour of Mans Saluacioune: A
Middle English Translation of 'Speculum humanae salvationis': A Critical
Edition of the Fifteenth-Century Manuscript Illustrated from* Der Spiegel
der menschen Behältnis, *Speyer: Drach, c.1475*, ed. Avril Henry (Aldershot:
Scolar Press and Philadelphia: University of Pennsylvania Press, 1986)
contains all the woodcuts illustrating *Speculum humanae salvationis* in the
printed Drach edition, where they occur among woodcuts illustrating other
texts with which the *Speculum* is there curiously interwoven.

known and widely distributed *Speculum humanae salvationis*.[2] The paper on which the *Mirour* manuscript is written is unusual in that its watermarks date the paper precisely as produced in Fabriano in 1429.[3] Its dialect is mixed—northern and north-east midland. The hand of the main scribe is of the first half of the fifteenth century, and the vocabulary suggests that the translation is unlikely to have been much earlier. Unfortunately, the manuscript's provenance is unknown before its ownership in about 1570 by a 'clerke' Thomas Cowper of 'Kylbury'.[4]

Chapter 39 of the *Mirour* begins with an account (lines 4105–4206) of how, after the Ascension, Christ showed his wounds to the Father in pleading for mankind, an event prefigured by Antipater's showing his wounds to Caesar.[5] The chapter goes on to describe how Christ's action is echoed also by the Virgin's showing her breasts to Christ in pleading for humankind, [6] and by Esther's pleading with King Ahasuerus for her people.[7] These events are presented as verbal images for meditative comparison, the simple relationships between the Types and Antetype being explained in the text. In many editions of *Speculum* the text is accompanied by illustrations of each scene. Fig. 1 (p. 183 below) shows these events as they appear in woodcuts illustrating a version of *Speculum* printed by Drach *c*.1475—the

2. Speculum Humanae Salvationis: *Texte critique traduction inédite de Jean Mielot (1448); les sources et l'influence iconographique principalement sur l'art alsacien du XIVe siècle: avec la reproduction, en 140 planches, du manuscrit de Sèlestat, de la série complète des vitraux de Mulhouse, de vitraux de Colmar, de Wissembourge, etc.*, ed. J. Lutz and P. Perdrizet, 2 vols (Mulhouse: Meininger, 1907, 1909).

3. *Mirour*, p. 20.

4. *Mirour*, pp. 20–23.

5. Petrus Comestor, *Historia scholastica*, PL 198:1531; see *The Mirour of Mans Saluacioune*, pp. 195 and 197, 4113–4172.

6. Ernald of Bonneval (d.1156) PL 189:1726. The image is recorded as rare in art until the influence of *Speculum humanae salvationis* was felt, but the thirteenth-century english Hereford Cathedral *mappa mundi* shows the scene at the top, where *The Last Judgement* is implied. The two images, of Christ and of the Virgin appealing for mankind, often appear conflated.

7. Est 5:3, 7:2–10.

Christ shows his wounds to the Father. Aquinas *ST* III q.54, a.4; John of Ford, Cant Serm 120.6.

The Virgin shows her breasts to her son. Ernald *PL* 189:1726.

Antipater shows his wounds to Caesar. Comestor 1531.

Esther pleads with her husband. Esther 5:3, 7:2–10.

Figure I: Woodcuts from the *Speculum humanae salvationis*

woodcuts which were used to illustrate the edition of the Middle English *Mirour* manuscript, which is unillustrated.[8]

The text of the *Mirour* with which we are concerned runs:

4107   Howe Crist his woundes to his Fader*e* shewes is to here fylowingly,
       And hir*e* blissid brestes to hir*e* son for vs shewes virgine Marie.
       Als Crist descendid to helle fro the heven for mankynde sake,
4110   So to heven is he reascendit, our*e* pees *with* his Fader*e* to make.
       We shuld noght falle in wanhope thogh we haf synned forthy,
       Having to the hevenyssh Fader*e* so trewe auokette and myghty.
4113   Th*at* Crist his cicatrices wold shewe his Fader*e* for vs,
       Tofore lange in figure was it p*re*ostendid thus:
       Antipat*er*, a noble knyght, was wryed to the emp*er*our Julian
4116   Th*at* he was wikked and vntrewe vnto the Empir*e* Roman,
       And he tyrved hym stone nakid, p*re*sent this emp*er*our*e*,
       Shewyng the erres of his woundes for thaym in many a stour*e*,
4119   And saide, 'What shuld my wordes p*ro*ve me wreche or worthy?
       . . .
4173   Crist to his Fader*e* shewes his cicatrices for mercy,
       And til hyr*e* son hir*e* bristes shewes for vs swete Marie.

In the right margin near lines 4113-14, which mean 'Christ's showing his wounds to his Father on our behalf was long ago prefigured thus', the main scribe wrote: 'B in Cant. last chap.' Again, at line 4173, near the line meaning 'Christ shows his wounds to the Father to obtain mercy [for us]' the scribe wrote in the left margin 'B*er*nard apon Cant*ica* vl*timo*' (my expansion is based on the fact that the reference is not to the last Canticle but to the last sermon) [See Figure 2, p. 184.]

None of St Bernard's homilies on Canticles refers to Christ's showing his wounds to the Father. The image is found in the last sermon of John's continuation of St Bernard on the Canticles which, on the evidence of this note, seems by the later Middle Ages to have been attributed to Bernard himself. The author of the image which

8. Avril Henry, 'The Woodcuts of *Der Spiegel menschlicher Behältnis* (*Speculum Humanae Salvationis*) in the Editions Printed by Drach and Richel,' *Oud Holland* 99.1 (1985) 1–15.

the annotator of *The Mirour of Mans Saluacioune* recalled will be referred to hereafter as John.

John addresses Christ thus:

> *Fuge ergo et excurre in coelestia, recurre in locum tuum, qui est omnipotentis Patris tui sinus. Exhibe Patri aeterno ma-nipulos oboedientiae tuae, et repraesenta ei passionis tuae signa uictricia, infer coelo gloriam crucis tuae; et sanguis tuus ille uiuificus pro ecclesia tua clamans uiscera paterna concutiat.*[9]

> Flee away, therefore, hasten forth to the things of heaven. Run home again to your own place, which is the bosom of your all-powerful Father. Display to your eternal Father the harvest of your obedience, bring vividly before him the victorious banners of your passion, bear into heaven the glory of your cross. Let your life's blood, crying aloud for your church, strike on the heart of your Father.[10]

The source of John's mention of obedience in this sermon lies in his Sermon 10:

> Then he who sat upon the throne gave orders that the huge sack containing all the sins of Adam and his sons, which had been sealed and hidden in the royal treasury, should be brought out into their midst. . . . The king said to his Son: 'You see before you the sack of your race, sealed.' . . . He finished speaking, and all who heard were lost in wonder at the willing obedience of such great majesty. The angels reeled in their seats and they began to say to one another: 'Truly this is the Son of God, for his very speech betrays him.'[11]

---

9. John of Forde, Cant Serm 120.6 (CCCM 17:809). The image's later popularity is attested by its appearance in Aquinas *ST* 3. q. 54. a. 4.

10. Wendy Mary Beckett, *John of Ford: Sermons on the Final Verses of the Song of Songs* 7, Cistercian Fathers Series 47 (Kalamazoo: Cistercian Publications, 1984) 246.

11. Cant Serm 10.3–5; CCM 17:96–98 (CF 29:193–196). Jesus's obedience is also treated in Cant Serm 9.7; 93, lines 202–224 (186–187).

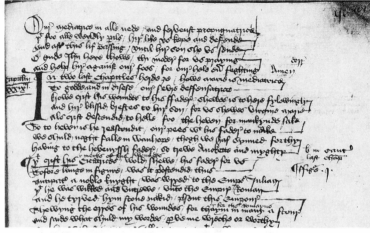

Fig. 2a The first reference, f. 50ʳ: 'B in Cant. last chapter'

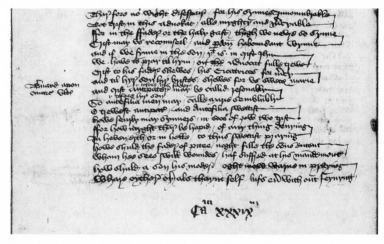

Fig. 2b The second reference, f.50ᵛ: 'Bernard apon Cantica vltimo'

Figure 2: The Mirour of Mans Saluacioune: The Marginal Reference

The scene imagined in Sermon 120 gives vivid visual form to the Atonement—the moment at which the Father accepts the Son's offering, the fruits of his obedience. However, the description of the scene may be more complex than it seems, for the phrase 'harvest of your obedience' (*manipulos obedientiae tuae*) seems to be a pun. That it is a deliberately created play on words, and not a mere ambiguity, is suggested by three factors. First, the image is curious: what has harvest to do with conquest? Why not use a word meaning 'spoils'? Second, if the evidence of the *index verborum* in the latin edition of John is a reliable guide, *manipulus* was not a word much used by him: only this example is cited.75

Third, *manipulus* carries many varied though connected connotations, and their connection may be relevant here.

The word's primary sense is 'handful (of hay, straw, etc.)'[12] or 'sheaf';[13] *manipulos* therefore seems to mean both 'handfuls'—the wounds themselves, visible in the hands which Christ extends to the Father—and 'harvest', referring to suffering indicated by those wounds. 'Spoils' would not carry this overlay of meaning. It seems likely that the quotation which John had in mind was Psalm 125:6, for this was sung on most days of the week at None and so would have had deep resonances for him, as it does for many monks to this day:

> Euntes ibant et flebant, mittentes semina sua,
> Venientes autem venient cum exultatione,

12. Lewis and Short, *A Latin Dictionary* (Oxford: Clarendon, 1879, repr. 1958). *A Lexicon of Ancient Latin Etymologies*, ARCA Classical and Medieval Texts: Papers and Monographs, 25 (Leeds: Francis Cairns, 1991) under *manipulus*, where the primary meaning is *fascis herbae*, cites Isidore, *Etymoliguae*, 17.9.10: 'manipulum *dicimus fascem faeni: et dictum* manipulum *quod manum inpleat*'.

13. The Vulgate uses *manipulos* eleven times. Usually it means 'sheaves', as in Gen 37.7 (*Putabam nos ligare manipulos in agro; et quasi consurgere manipulum meum, et stare, vestrosque manipulos circumstantes adorare manipulum meum*); see also Gen 41:47; Lev 23:10, 23:12, 23:15; Deut 24:19; Ruth 3:7; Judith 8:3; Ps 125:6, 128:7. The word means 'handfuls' where gleaning is the context, in Ruth 2:16 (*et de vestris quoque manipulis proiicite de industria*).

Portantes manipulos suos.[14]

Those who go out weeping,
bearing the seed for sowing,
shall come home with shouts of joy
carrying their sheaves

(NRSV)

It may even be relevant that *manipulos* has military connotations:
as Isidore observes in his explanation of the word *Vexillum*: '*Sub
Romulo autem fasciculos feni, pro vexillis, milites habuerunt. Hinc
et manipuli appellantur.* Manipulos *enim dicimus fasces feni, quod
manum impleant.*'[15] As the passage is about victory ('the victorious
banners of your passion '), perhaps this association is also present.
One thinks of the ancient hymn:

> *Vexilla Regis prodeunt;*
> *Fulget Crucis mysterium*
> *Qua vita mortem pertulit*
> *Et morte vitam protulit.*
> *Quae vulnerata lanceae*
> *Mucrone diro, criminum*
> *Ut nos lavaret sordibus*
> *Manavit unda et sanguine.*

The elusive link between hands, harvest, and victory seems to be
located in the origins of *manipulos* itself.

---

14. I am much indebted to Hilary Costello for pointing out the significance of Ps 125:6 here, for making the cross-reference to Sermon 10,
and for pointing out Bernard's parallel use of *manipulos* in his Sermon
37.4 *Super Cantica: Felix qui tantum iam messuit, habens interim quidem
fructum suum in sanctificationem, finem vero vitam aeternum! Merito qui
se invento flevit, gavisus est viso Domino, ad cuius utique miserationis
intuitum tantos iam levavit manipulos, remissionem, sanctificationem, spem
vitae. O quam verus est sermo qui in Propheta legitur: Qui seminant in
lacrimis, in exsultatione metent* (SBOp 2:11).
15. *Etymol.*, 18.3.5 (PL 83:643).

In addition, it may be that contemporary readers would make the imaginative leap from 'handfuls of hay' to the image of Christ bearing the most un-hay-like nails of the Cross projecting from his palms like horns—the parallel deriving from Habakkuk 3: 4: *Cornua in manibus eius; / Ibi abscondita est fortitudo eius* ('There are horns on his hands: there his strength is hidden').[16]

Manipulos carries still further implications. It may mean 'maniples', the stylized hand-towels which in the Mass signify the symbolic wiping away of impurity from the priest's hands before he handles the host.[17] If that sense is present here, it perhaps signifies that Christ's wounds purify humankind in Christ's flesh, in preparation for humankind's reunion with God. Finally, *manipulos* in the sense of the vestment 'maniples' may suggest the clothing of Christ's body in his 'life-giving blood'—the blood symbolized by the red vestments worn on the feasts of martyrs. The mind of the author of the *Speculum*, certainly, turns next towards the familiar image of Christ's blood-stained clothing, for as the *Mirour* says shortly afterwards:

4129 That Oure Lord Jhesu Crist was knyght noble and worthy
      Shewed in his cicatrices and in his clothing blody:
      Fore rede sangvinolent was alle ouer Cristis clothing,

4132 Like to clothes of the men of rede wyne grapes treding;
      Wharefore of Cristis clothis thus askid aungels dyvine
      Whi thai ware rede als of men out of grapes stampyng the wyne.

4135 'The pressoure of my passioune tholid I alle one,' quod he,
'And of alle folk in erth was noght o man with me.'[18]

Whatever the original resonances of *manipulos obedientiae tuae*, the *Mirour*'s marginal reference to the last sermon of John's contin-

16. The verse is one of the prophecies of the crucifixion in *Biblia Pauperum*, sig. .e. (Henry, pp. 96, 98). Gertrud Schiller, *Iconography of Christian Art*, Vol.2, trans. Janet Seligman from the 2nd ed. (London: Lund Humphries, 1972) fig. 485, shows a crucifix in which Christ's hands *held in front of him* have horn-like nails projecting from them—though this object is fourteenth-century.

17. *Novum glossarium*, *manipulus* sense 4.

18. *The Mirour of Mans Saluacioune*, p. 195,4129–135. See Is 63:1–3; the Mystic Winepress is discussed in Schiller, 228–29.

uation of St Bernard on the Canticles raises a number of interesting topics for a large research project, perhaps for specialists in cistercian studies.

- How early and how common was the literary image? Did John invent or transmit it? It is hard to believe the former, yet the image's art history does not suggest a patristic source—at least not a well-known one: the earliest visual presentations of *Christ Shows His Wounds to the Father* are apparently in fourteenth-century manuscripts of *Speculum*.[19]
- If no source for the image is known to predate John, does its presence in *Speculum* imply that the latter is a cistercian text?
- If the origin of *Speculum* is Italian or German, does this tell us anything about the reading of John in early fourteenth-century Europe?
- Do any surviving copies of *Speculum* bear marginalia associating the image with John? Lutz and Perdrizet do not refer to such a reference in any of the copies which they collated for their edition. If the *Mirour* scribe did find the John reference in a Latin copy, recognition of the source may have occurred almost anywhere in western Europe, where *Speculum* was in wide circulation.
- Do any of the surviving copies of *Speculum* known to have been made in England carry the John reference?
- Does the presence of the 'Bernard' reference in the *Mirour* imply that the Middle English translation was cistercian? In the Latin *Prohemium* (unfortunately not published by Lutz and Perdrizet), the summary of the thirty-seventh chapter refers, as does the chapter it summarizes, to the vision granted *beato patri Dominico*, in which Dominic saw the Virgin intercede to prevent God throwing his three spears of justice at mankind. It is well known that in its translation of the *Prohemium* (but not in its main text) the Middle English substitutes Benedict for Dominic:

250   The seven and threttith, how Oure Ladie excused this world to hire son,

---

19. Schiller, 3, shows some derivatives of the *Speculum* image but does not mention any source for them in the Fathers, and she is usually assiduous in these matters.

Als sometyme to Seinte Benet was shwed in avision,
When Oure Lord toward this werld shoke thre speres
wrothly,
And Oure Ladie putt hir betwix and turned his ire to mercy.

English cistercian interest in typological compendia is well-known:
the largest, the thirteenth-century English *Pictor in carmine*, is
named after the self-description given by the Cistercian who wrote
it.[20]

- If it could be shown that recognition of 'Christ Shows His
  Wounds to the Father' as used by John was not to be attributed
  to the *Mirour's* translator but to its unknown and only roughly
  located northern or north-east midland scribe (though I cannot
  imagine how, since we have only the one Middle English copy
  of the work, and its fifteenth-century provenance is virtually
  unknown), would that reveal anything useful about the reading
  of John in late medieval England?

Perhaps responses to these questions will be made easier by a brief
account of the devotional context in which the John image is used—
the shape and nature of the *Speculum* itself. The author of the
Speculum is unknown. The earliest surviving manuscript is, if Evelyn
Silber is correct, *c*.1310.[21] The original was therefore probably of
the late thirteenth century. Its country of origin is contested, with
Italy and Germany formerly leading the field. The work's great
popularity is evident in the very large number of *Speculum* manuscripts surviving—over 394, many of them fully and expensively
illustrated[22]—and by the fact that the book was among the earliest

20. T. J. Brown, 'Pictor in carmine,' *British Museum Quarterly*, 19 1954,
73–5; M. R. James, 'Pictor in carmine,' *Archeologia* 94, 1951, 141–66, gives
only the List of Contents of this vast work.

21. Evelyn Silber, 'The Reconstructed Toledo *Speculum Humanae Salvationis*: The Italian Connection in the Early Fourteenth Century,' *Journal
of the Warburg and Courtauld Institutes* 43, 1980, 32–51, and 'The Early
Iconography of the *Speculum Humanae Salvationis*: The Italian Connection
in the Early Fourteenth Century.' Diss. Cambridge 1982.

22. See Speculum humanae salvationis: *Vollständige Faksimileausgabe
des Codex Cremifanensis 243 des Benediktinerstifts Kremsmunster*, ed.
W. Neumüller, 2 vols (Graz: Akademische Druck-u. Verlagsanstalt, 1972).

to be printed, in blockbook (woodcut) form and in a mixture of woodcut and set type. Its distribution was wide: it survives in texts written in Latin, German, French, Dutch, Czech and English; Silber believes the Toledo copy to be Italian in origin.[23]

The book is in forty-five chapters. Chapters 1-2 present an abbreviated Old Testament background to salvation, up to Noah's Ark. Chapters 3–42 each consist of one hundred lines; they present the summary life of the Virgin in which is embedded the life, death, resurrection and ascension of Christ. The method, as in the *Biblia Pauperum* which is *Speculum*'s forerunner and occasionally its source,[24] is typological, but whereas the former foreshadows each Antitype or New Law event (usually from the New Testament) by two Types or prefigurations (usually from the Old Testament), *Speculum* offers three Types to each Antitype, as in Fig. 1 above. Chapters 43-45, each containing 208 lines, are not typological, but form three sets of devotions related to the seven canonical hours. Each of these three chapters consists of an introduction, a visionary tale, and a set of Hours—of the Passion, the Seven Sorrows and the Seven Joys of the Virgin.

There is both a *Prohemium* (a summary) and a Prologue for the *Speculum*. In the *Prohemium*, the author (or rather an author, for it cannot be proved that it was the book's creator who wrote the main text) explained, in a latin passage not translated in the Middle English,[25] that his summary (*not*, as is often reported, the main work) was made 'for the sake of poor preachers, so that if by any chance they cannot afford to buy the whole book they can, if they know the stories, preach from the Prohemium itself.' Unambiguous evidence of use of the summary or book in sermons— a use possibly distinct from the book's original purpose—would be welcome, but the structure of the book itself, ending as it does with

23. Evelyn Silber, 'The Reconstructed Toledo *Speculum humanae salvationis*,' 32–51.

24. Biblia Pauperum: *A Facsimile and Edition [of the Forty-page Blockbook Version]*. Ed. Avril Henry. London: Scolar, 1987; Ithaca: Cornell, 1987.

25. *The Mirour of Mans Saluacioune*, Appendix, p. 227.

Hours, seems to suggest that its main functions are devotional and meditational.

It is unfortunate that the Prologue does not appear in the *Mirour*,[26] for it offers 'both laymen and clerics' a rare and endearing contemporary account of the uses, limitations and dangers of typology:

> For example, although Absolom wickedly took revenge on his father, neverthless Christ is prefigured by him on account of some similiarities—not because Absolom treated his father badly, but because he was the most beautiful of men and was hanged on a tree: for Christ was 'beautiful above the sons of men and hanged from the tree of the Cross.'

Typology must be interpreted judiciously, the author explains, as the monks of a monastery take only what each needs from an oak tree felled in their courtyard.[27]

This paper should perhaps be treated in a similar manner, readers taking from it what suits their needs. It appears to suggest a late medieval English readership for John. As an analysis of an image from John it may contribute a mite to the understanding of John's style. As an outline of research opportunities, it may serve at least to place John of Forde, *Speculum humanae salvationis* and *The Mirour of Mans Saluacioune* in a new relationship to each other.

26. *The Mirour of Mans Saluacioune*, pp. 227–28 offer a modern english translation.

27. A miniature from the *Speculum humanae salvationis* Bibliothèque Nationale MS Fr.6275, f.1ᵛ, illustrating his extended simile of the felled tree, appears on the cover of *The Mirour of Mans Saluacioune*, where it has puzzled readers who have not consulted the Appendix or the back flap of the dust cover.

Beverly Aitken, OCSO _____

John of Forde
Twelfth Century Guide for Twentieth Century Monk

GREGORY THE GREAT wrote in 580 of pastors who 'make affection for themselves as a sort of road by which to lead the hearts of their hearers to love of the Creator and who draw others by the sweetness of their own characters to affection for the truth.'[1] In this paper I hope to show how John of Ford, having won my affection and become a 'sort of road' for me, serves as a guide to the twentieth-century monk. No doubt, John would welcome affably any of us who might choose him as a spiritual guide!

What kind of person was John of Ford? He has been described as a man of 'unfailing courtesy and charm,' a 'master of the spiritual life,'[2] 'a wise and holy writer' and 'very much a man for our time.'[3] I find him a lovably generous and passionate person, whose sermons are peppered with superlatives: 'fully,' 'wholly,' 'always,' 'never'. Paul is healed, for example, not by a 'look from Jesus' but by a 'long look from Jesus.'[4] Again, it is not just the 'silence' of the infant Christ, but 'the thunder of his silence.'[5] John is sure of himself, sure of his teaching, profoundly prayerful and humble. He seems to have

1. *Pastoral Rule*, Part II, ch. 8.
2. Hilary Costello, 'John of Ford', *Cistercian Studies Quarterly* 13/1 (1978) 47.
3. Wendy Mary Beckett in the 'Translator's Preface', *John of Ford: Sermons on the Song of Songs* 1 (=CF 29):64.
4. Serm 9.4 (1:183).
5. Serm 9.4 (1:183).

a deep intuition of the mutuality of the divine-human relationship—what God does to us we do to God. In Sermon 50, for example, he says of Christ: 'He is dissatisfied with eating us unless he too in his turn should be eaten by us.'[6]

John saw himself, I believe, above all, as a spiritual guide: 'To work for your growth in virtue—it was for this that you chose me as your abbot.'[7] He is a spiritual guide whose effectiveness flows from burning experience. By his enthusiasm he sweeps us into his own fire of ardent devotion to the kenotic Christ, pleading in charming self-effacement, 'Do not pay such attention to what I am in myself that you refuse to accept my service. I beg you, come close to the fire.'[8]

I have said that John of Ford's effectiveness as a spiritual guide can be credited to the depths of his own experience; now his experience is of his relationship to the Christ who is humble and poor. In speaking of the Lord's birth, John observes: 'Since you were a little one, you made yourself like all little ones in weakness, except that you stood out as a more ardent seeker after littleness.'[9] Such was his birth, but even now when—as the Easter liturgy puts it—'all power and dominion are his' '. . . he remains always the same in his humility, and the years of Jesus' poverty and lowliness will never come to an end.'[10] And: 'He is the first and his glory is above the heavens, and yet at the same time he is the last, and his humility is lower than the very lowest of the lowly.'[11]

Among the cistercian writers it is John's special gift to have pierced the secret of Christ's interiority: his self-emptying. The glory of the Risen One is to serve. In heaven itself amidst all the saints, 'Christ Jesus goes before them and is their servant . . . as he passes he serves them with utmost humble reverence.'[12]

6. Serm 50.4 (4:47).
7. Serm 61.1 (4:196).
8. Serm 108.1 (7:93).
9. Serm 9.2 (1:181).
10. Serm 4.2 (1:114).
11. Serm 36.1 (3:85).
12. Serm 85.8 (6:34).

This focus on Christ's self-emptying accounts for much of John's appeal today. Is it not significant that only now, in the trauma and upheaval of this century some eight hundred years after their composition, his sermons have come to light? The poverty and humility of Christ exercise a powerful attraction for our contemporaries who agonize in Gethsemanes of our time and place: Hiroshima, Dachau, Bangladesh, Baghdad. Ruth Burrows comments in her *Guidelines to Mystical Prayer*:

> Every age . . . has its own understanding of Jesus . . . . Is it possible to say what particular aspect of the Incarnation is holding (people's) hearts today and shaping their lives . . . ? I would venture that it is precisely that of Christ crucified in weakness . . . . Now we grasp that in fact he . . . experienced to the depths what it means to be (human) . . . unprivileged, helpless . . . like us in all things.[13]

How is the monk-disciple to respond to the spirit of Jesus, a 'spirit all gentle and humble?' John would urge the obviously appropriate response: 'humility, the mother of all virtues.'[14] For 'humility is enormously strong'; it is 'all justice'.[15] 'How great a virtue humility is. The Holy Spirit makes it fruitful . . . the higher it becomes, the lowlier it strives to be.'[16] It is 'true and heavenly freedom,' 'healing,' 'true glory,' 'great beauty.'[17] For John, humility is a response to what the Holy Spirit is doing in the heart of the monk: 'Because of Jesus, he makes his soul subject to every human creature, not only to his fathers and equals, but even to his . . . juniors.'[18] Everything is to be judged in humility's light: 'Let us not consider anything menial if it urges us to lowliness and instructs us in humility.'[19]

13. Ruth Burrows, *Guidelines for Mystical Prayer* (Denville, N.J., 1980) p. 4.
14. Serm 73.5 (5:135).
15. Serm 9.1 and 51.4 (1:177; 4:62).
16. Serm 51.9 (4:67–8).
17. Serm 76.4: 36.2: 79.4: 49.10 (5:174; 3:86; 5:214; 4:40).
18. Serm 110.8 (7:124).
19. Serm 89.11 (6:81).

It is a sign of love: 'The soul that loves Jesus . . . is very zealous for humility,' knowing that 'it is only on the small and lowly that Jesus looks or the Spirit rests.'[20] It is a monk's very profession:

> But I tell you, brothers, our profession is humility. Everything that has to do with our outward behavior, the habit we show to the world, the mutual encounter whenever brother meets brother, the mutual reverence when brothers sit down together, the readiness to obey, and all the other marks of humility which our forebears recommended to us . . . . But there must be a desire for inward humility . . . so that all the humble behavior we profess is voluntary, coming forth from the pasture of a fruitful heart. . . . [21]

For anyone called to serve his or her brothers or sisters in a pastoral office, John provides an eminent role model. He knows that 'those who are in authority over others need greater holiness' and 'deeper lovingkindness', for 'to be in charge of others means inescapable anxiety'.[22] If we were to ask John's opinion as to the indispensable condition for a spiritual father's or mother's fruitfulness, he would probably reply as he wrote in Sermon 50:

> If anyone desires to shear me into poverty and patience so that I may learn from him to become poor and naked . . . . then he must first practice what he is preaching. If he is to shear without hindrance, then first let him be sheared himself.[23]

Then he would advise those who labor for the souls of others to return to the source of their strength—that is, to prayer. John would have them 'gaze silently on the Word'.[24]

20. Serm 51.5: 19.2 (4:62; 2:62).
21. Serm 51.10 (4:68).
22. Serm 50.9: 51.5 (4:53, 63).
23. Serm 50.5 (4:50).
24. Serm 99.2 (6:203).

... even as [the sun] was bestowed upon the world by God to give light, it still ought to turn aside fairly frequently, to have a time for peace and quiet . . . . it ought to know how to set and be at rest in the evening, when it enters the embrace of leisure.[25]

John understands the difficulty of the shepherd's role: 'The one who . . . suffers the loss of his own spiritual ease for the profit of another . . . surely follows the example of the Saviour, giving his soul as the price of redemption for many . . . .'[26] But he would not have been caught up in our concern over burnout!

When your household sits down to a meal, if you are wise, you will first sit down yourself, and then you will be able to serve them easily and happily. In your charity to your neighbor, remember that your nearest neighbor is yourself.[27]

John hints at the state of integration which will eventually come to such pastors: 'for a soul so taken up with interior occupation, activity and rest have become the same thing', while he does not neglect to warn those who 'are entirely given over to exterior concerns and can scarcely endure taking a deep breath in the depths of their souls or ever recollecting themselves . . . . This is not how the Bride acts . . . . It is on [Jesus], whatever her exterior occupations may be, that she constantly keeps her eyes . . . .'[28]

If humility and prayer are part of the pastoral store, so too is compassion. John shares the present-day abbot's care to identify with his monks. As he puts it, 'It is their duty to live among sheep as simply one of them'.[29] Like the desert father who healed Theopemptus by revealing his own struggles, John can readily admit his needs:

25. Serm 57.11–12 (4:151).
26. Serm 115.3 (7:182).
27. Serm 71.4 (5:110).
28. Serm 91.1: 89.9–10 (6:98: pp. 78, 80).
29. Serm 50.7 (4:51).

> I recall my coldness, which sometimes benumbs my heart
> into a state of torpor . . . . There is alive in me some tiny
> flame of your love . . . . But I have no power at all to blow
> it into flame unless your Spirit . . . comes to the help of my
> weakness.[30]

Again he confesses his inadequacies as he apologizes for expounding the mysteries of Scripture 'knowing only too well that in supplies of this substance, "I am poor and needy" '. Even at the conclusion of his task John insists that he has spoken 'from the utter poverty of my heart'.[31] The phrase is reminiscent of Thomas Merton's 'I have become the poverty of God'.[32]

Weaknesses, however, did not lead John to discouragement, for he knew that these can work for our benefit. For him, that is, our own weakness is like a wick in a lamp. It makes us humble, and that humility is like oil which gives light and heat to make the soul on fire with longing for God's love and God's love clothes the soul in the light of wisdom.[33]

In touch as he was with his own need, John is able to show affectionate tenderness for frailty and to inspire perseverance in even the most timid disciple. He understood that the Bride herself has passed through difficulties, aridities, trials: ' . . . she recalls with eager heart where she came from and where he has now brought her, and it seems to her that, in the middle of the underworld, Jesus is with her.'[34]

In identifying with his flock as he does, John does not forget to provide nourishment for them—indeed, to become himself that nourishment. 'A pastor gets his name by never neglecting his duty of providing pasture.'[35] The flocks are those 'whom they should be leading to pasture and for whom they should be pasture.'[36]

30. Serm 86.1 (6:37).
31. Serm 120.8 (7:249)
32. Thomas Merton, *Woods, Shore, Desert* (Santa Fe: Museum of New Mexico Press, 1982) p. 24.
33. Serm 108.6 (7:97).
34. Serm 80.9 (5:230).
35. Serm 112.2 (7:143–144)
36. Serm 103.4 (7:35).

John's humility, prayer, and loving compassion are the more welcome as they are offered to his monks, and to us, with the quiet humor and lightness of touch that make an appearance right in the Prologue. Setting forth his purpose, for example, in commenting on the Song of Songs, he compares himself to a cold cook: 'for those who work in the kitchen there is a fire close at hand. . . .' A few lines on, he apologizes for the 'length of this work . . . though at this stage remorse comes rather late!'[37] Again he pokes fun at himself: 'we have become like the meekest of asses. . . .'[38] Elsewhere, speaking of Christ's cheekbone, he makes use of the word *asinus* in a playful pun: *in maxilla non asinina sed propria, immo vere asinina quia propria*[39]

Related to his sense of humor is John's penchant for the 'pithy aphorism'. Those of us who have no patience with prolixity are caught off guard at their sudden flash in a tangle of verbal undergrowth and find ourselves enticed to read on. Consider these, for example: 'Those who love the name of Jesus . . . know only peace.' 'Charity has no desire . . . but . . . to be a humble emptiness that God will fill.' 'What begins in love cannot but end there.'[40]

Once our interest has been awakened in this way, we can draw on John's fund of practical wisdom in the ways of seeking God. I would like to give one example of his practicality by referring to Sermon One where he explains to the person 'whose sole need is to seek him' three ways of looking for Jesus.[41] The first of these ways is to seek him through vigils—that is, prayer at night—'since the Spouse is wont to appear while all things are in silence in the middle of the night'. When this fails ('laboring all night, she catches nothing'), the soul seeks Jesus through pastoral service to others. 'For she knows that Jesus draws near to those who speak of him, and that in the breaking of bread, which is the Word of God, he commonly reveals the face of his glory. . . .' The third kind of seeking is 'that of humble listening in silence'—'for to reward listening more copiously than

37. Serm Prol. 6 (1:73–4).
38. Serm 18.7 (2:55).
39. Serm 53.1 (4:83).
40. Serm 30.1: 24.7: 47.10 (3:14; 2:143; 4:14).
41. Serm 1.3 (1:81).

speaking is his way. . . .' Apparently this third way of seeking must meet with success, for John describes the coming of Jesus, at last. 'He . . . fulfills the desire of all who fear him — how much more of those who love him. . . .' [42]

There is no seeking Jesus without faith, and later John is to insist that we penetrate beneath the surface: 'Infirmities especially of the body are as it were the garments of the Lord Jesus. Dwelling in these pelts and clad in this kind of garment, what he wishes is to ask us a question: whether we truly know and love him so disguised.'[43] John is aware that special trials arise from the very nature of community life. He passes on to us the commonsense quotation: 'I feel it is better to yield to another than to be the slave of contention.'[44] Suffering is to be accepted in the context of faith's surer vision: 'Take confidently as from a Father's hand, the cup which your Father has given you as his fatherly gift. . . . Take care not to describe as wickedly forced on you by your brother what is in fact graciously tendered by your Father.'[45] Just as Jesus himself 'did not take this chalice from the hand of Pilate . . . No, he accepted it eagerly as offered to him by his Father, and he gladly drained it.'[46]

John points out that 'Any soul . . . that longs for the joys of love must not shrink back from its bitterness if (the soul) desires to experience its sweetness.'[47] The key that unlocks the door to these joys is love of Jesus crucified: 'For any soul that loves the Lord Jesus, or wants to love him . . . set Jesus and him crucified as a seal upon your heart.'[48] Can the ordinary monk emulate the Bride who is so often held up as an example of this love? For the Bride is one who 'loves deeply, who burns with love . . . who chooses to know nothing except Jesus alone.'[49]

42. Serm 1.2–3 (1:79–82).
43. Serm 6.9–10 (1:144–145).
44. Serm 8.4 (1:167).
45. Serm 4.7 (1:121).
46. Serm 76.7 (5:177).
47. Serm 24.5 (2:139).
48. Serm 105.9 (7:63).
49. Serm 81.9 (5:240).

None of us, however, need be intimidated by the fact that the Bride has advanced far beyond us in the ways of prayer. John would encourage us by showing us that the Bride, even though her 'sole occupation be to gaze on the face of Jesus',[50] is not perhaps far removed from our own journey. We may not yet be able to see ourselves as someone 'who clings to God with . . . the utmost earnestness and a single-minded intensity', but still we can hope to identify with the Bride as 'someone who has only just begun to love' or as one whom Jesus 'intends to heal by nothing less than the favor of his kiss and the sweet breathing of his Spirit.'[51] The Bride's love for Jesus is not her own achievement. '[She] has been made all loving by the loving gaze of her Beloved.'[52] For 'he sanctifies by his touch and look all who approach him.'[53]

No matter how enviable the Bride's relationship with Jesus, I suspect that for John it is not enough only to know Jesus, that the soul does not really know him until it has been wounded by him. And this wound is to be sought after: 'Who would not freely run forward to be wounded, making a willing and zealous offering of his soul to receive the wound of a love so great? In my case, I beseech you, do not hold back, O Lord my God, . . . do not treat me mildly!'[54] It is, however, a mutual wounding, for the Bride's beauty 'wounds his heart . . . enters into the very depths of his being.'[55] 'Someone has touched me, said Jesus . . . So it is good to touch him [by faith] . . . but far better to wound him with the thrust of love. . . .'[56]

How illuminating it is to compare Baldwin of Forde's analytical and impersonal tractate on the wounds[57] with John of Ford's passionate treatment of this theme. John has tasted Christ in his reading:

50. Serm 68.8 (5:84).
51. Serm 63.2: 61.10: 24.8 (5:14; 4;204; 2:144).
52. Serm 91.2 (6:99).
53. Serm 119.2 (7:230).
54. Serm 33.7 (3:56).
55. Serm 51.3 (4:60).
56. Serm 48.9 (4:26 emended).
57. Baldwin of Ford, Tractate VIII in *Spiritual Tractates*, Vol 1, Cistercian Fathers Series, Vol. 39, Trans. David N. Bell (Kalamazoo: Cistercian Publications, 1986) 214f.

'Your word . . . still hidden from the eyes of our understanding . . . has already wounded the heart'[58] and, like Origen, he has gazed on the beauty of that Word in prayer: 'A mighty sword, Lord Jesus, is your splendor and beauty . . . a sword of flame . . . it admits none to true happiness unless he be first transfixed and consumed by sacred fire.'[59] Wounded by the love of Christ, John is able to 'set others alight with the same fire and wound them with a like hurt.'[60]

It seems to me that in his cistercian vocation to humility of heart, John has been brought to the very center of his own nothingness and rests there with Jesus. A monk of our own day who follows John's way to Christ will find in him a sure guide and will be able to make his or her own this prayer of John of Forde:

> . . . never let me be drawn away from you until you have given me fully to drink and be intoxicated by you, and until you have flowed down upon me like a river of peace.[61]

58. Serm 22.1 (2:102).
59. *Commentary on the Song of Songs*, Ancient Christian Writers series, Vol. 26 (New York: Newman Press) 199, 297. John, Serm 4.1 (1:112).
60. Serm 1.6 (1:85–6).
61. Serm 105.7 (7:61).

Select Bibliography
of the Works on John of Forde

Editions and translations:

The Life of Wulfric: *Wulfric of Haselbury by John, Abbot of Ford,*
ed. Maurice Bell (Somerset Record Society, XLVII 1933). Par-
tial translation by Pauline Matarasso in *The Cistercian World:
Monastic Writings of the Twelfth Century* (Penguin Books, Har-
mondsworth, 1993) pp. 235–273. Full translation by †Eugene
Green and Beverly Mayne Kienzle, forthcoming from Cistercian
Publications.

The Commentary on the Song of Songs: *Iohannis de Forda Super
Extremam Partem Cantici Canticorum Sermones CXX,* edd. Ed-
mund Mikkers and Hilary Costello, CCCM 17–18. Turnholt:
Brepols, 1970. Translated by Wendy Mary Beckett, *John of Ford
Sermons on the Final Verses of the Song of Songs,* 7 vols, CF 29,
39, 43–47. Kalamazoo, 1977–1984.

The Sermon for Palm Sunday: 'Un sermon inédit de Jean de Ford',
ed. anon (C. H. Talbot), *Collectanea Ordinis Cisterciensium
Reformatorum,* 7 (1940–45) pp. 36–45.

Secondary works published since 1970:

Hilary Costello, 'The Idea of the Church in the Sermons of John of
Ford', *Cîteaux* 21 (1970) 236–264.

———, 'John of Ford and the Quest for Wisdom', *Cîteaux* 23 (1972) 141–159.

———, 'Hesychasm in the English Cistercians of the Twelfth and Thirteenth Centuries', in *One Yet Two*, ed. M. Basil Pennington, Cistercian Studies 29. Kalamazoo, 1976. Pp. 332–351.

———, 'John of Ford', *Cistercian Studies [Quarterly]* 13 (1978) 46–67.

———, 'The Rule of Saint Benedict in Some English Cistercian Fathers', *Regula Benedicti Studia* 6–7. Hildesheim, 1981. Pp. 123–147.

———, 'The Secret of God in John of Ford', *Hallel* 11 (1983) 80–89.

———, 'The Holy Spirit: A Real Person in Our Lives', *Cistercian Studies [Quarterly]* 21 (1986) 325–344.

A. D., 'John of Ford, Commentary on the Latter Part of the Song of Songs', *Cîteaux* 21 (1970) 105–110.

Christopher Holdsworth, '*Another Stage . . . a different world*': *Ideas and People around Exeter in the Twelfth Century*. University of Exeter, 1979.

———, 'Frühe zisterziensische Spiritualität in Forde', *Die Zisterzienser: Ordensleben zwischen Ideal und Wirklichkeit. Ergänzungsband*, edd. Kaspar Elm and Peter Joerißen. Cologne 1982. Pp. 61–70.

———. 'The Cistercians in Devon', in *Studies in Medieval History presented to R. Allen Brown*, edd. Christopher Harper-Bill, Christopher Holdsworth and Janet L. Nelson. Woodbridge, 1989. Pp. 179–192.

———, 'Hermits and the Powers of the Frontier', in *Saints and Saints' Lives*, Reading Medieval Studies 16 (1990) 55–76.

———, 'From 1050 to 1307', in *Unity and Variety. A History of the Church in Devon and Cornwall*, ed. Nicholas Orme, Exeter Studies in History 29. Exeter University Press, 1991. Pp. 23–52.

E. McCorkell, 'Herald of the Holy Spirit: John of Ford's Sermons on the Song of Songs', *Cistercian Studies [Quarterly]* 20 (1985) 303–313.

Edmund Mikkers, 'Image and Likeness: The Doctrine of John of Ford', in *One Yet Two*, ed. M. Basil Pennington, Cistercian Studies 29. Kalamazoo, 1976. Pp. 352–356.

————, 'The Christology of John of Ford' in *Cistercian Ideals and Reality*, ed. John R. Sommerfeldt, Cistercian Studies 60. Kalamazoo, 1978. Pp. 220–244.

————, 'Jean de Ford', *Dictionnaire de Spiritualité* 8 (1988) cols. 516–527.

Elizabeth Oxenham, 'Under the Apple Tree': A Comparative Exegesis of Song of Songs 2:3 in the Sermons by Bernard of Clairvaux and John of Ford', *Bernardus Magister*, ed. John R. Sommerfeldt, Cistercian Studies 135. Kalamazoo, 1992. Pp. 277–286.

————, 'Appreciation of the Feminine in the Sermons of John of Ford on the Canticle' (forthcoming).

Notes on Contributors

Beverly Aitken is abbess of the cistercian community of Santa Rita Abbey in Sonoita, Arizona. She entered the Cistercian Order at Mount Saint Mary's Abbey in Wrentham, Massachusetts in 1961, and went with the founding sisters to Arizona eleven years later.

David Bell is Professor of Religious Studies at the Memorial University of Newfoundland where he teaches comparative religion. He holds degrees from Oxford University and from Leeds University. In recent years he has published extensively on the library holdings of medieval English religious houses and has written two introductions to doctrinal development within Christianity.

Hilary Costello is a cistercian monk of Mount Saint Bernard Abbey in Leicestershire, and one of the editors of the critical latin edition of the sermons of John of Forde. He serves the monastic community as bursar and does counselling with guests.

Marsha Dutton is Professor of English at Hanover College, Hanover, Indiana. She did her doctoral studies at the University of Michigan, where she also worked on the Middle English Dictionary and taught before taking her present position. Dr Dutton has published extensively on Aelred of Rievaulx and on Middle English religious writers.

Avril Henry is Professor of English Medieval Culture in the School of English of the University of Exeter.

Christopher Holdsworth is Professor Emeritus of Medieval History at the University of Exeter, where he specialized in the history of religious orders, especially the Cistercians. An active member of the Society of Friends, he is also a Trustee of the Joseph Rowntree Charitable Trust, a cellist in the Exeter Symphony, and the organizer of the John of Forde Symposium.

Pauline Matarasso is a scholar and translator living in Oxford. She holds advanced degrees from both Oxford and Paris and has published extensively on medieval french literature, especially the chivalric grail literature and its theology. Her anthology of twelfth-century cistercian writings, *The Cistercian World*, was published by Penguin in 1993.

Elizabeth Oxenham is a member of the community of Holy Cross Abbey, Whitland. An Australian by birth, she entered the Cistercian Order at Holy Cross Abbey when it was located at Stapehill, Dorset, which had been founded as a refuge for continental nuns after the French Revolution. She now lives very near the site of the first cistercian abbey in Wales.

Index Of Persons

205

Index Of Places

Subject Index

The editors express their appreciation to
Finbarr Donovan for creating the indices.

CISTERCIAN PUBLICATIONS, INC.
TITLES LISTING

—CISTERCIAN TEXTS—

THE WORKS OF
BERNARD OF CLAIRVAUX

Apologia to Abbot William
Five Books on Consideration: Advice to a Pope
Homilies in Praise of the Blessed Virgin Mary
The Life and Death of Saint Malachy the Irishman
Love without Measure. Extracts from the Writings
    of St Bernard (Paul Dimier)
On Grace and Free Choice
On Loving God (Emero Stiegman)
The Parables of Saint Bernard (Michael Casey)
Sermons for the Summer Season
Sermons on Conversion
Sermons on the Song of Songs I - IV
The Steps of Humility and Pride

THE WORKS OF
WILLIAM OF SAINT THIERRY

The Enigma of Faith
Exposition on the Epistle to the Romans
Exposition on the Song of Songs
The Golden Epistle
The Mirror of Faith
The Nature of Dignity of Love
On Contemplating God, Prayer & Meditations

THE WORKS OF AELRED OF RIEVAULX

Dialogue on the Soul
Liturgical Sermons, I
The Mirror of Charity
Spiritual Friendship
Treatises I: On Jesus at the Age of Twelve, Rule for a
    Recluse, The Pastoral Prayer
Walter Daniel: The Life of Aelred of Rievaulx

THE WORKS OF JOHN OF FORD

Sermons on the Final Verses of the Songs of Songs
    I - VII

THE WORKS OF GILBERT OF HOYLAND

Sermons on the Songs of Songs I-III
Treatises, Sermons and Epistles

OTHER EARLY CISTERCIAN WRITERS

The Letters of Adam of Perseigne I
Alan of Lille: The Art of Preaching
Baldwin of Ford: Spiritual Tractates I - II
Gertrud the Great of Helfta: Spiritual Exercises
Gertrud the Great of Helfta: The Herald of God's
    Loving-Kindness
Guerric of Igny: Liturgical Sermons I -[II]
Idung of Prüfening: Cistercians and Cluniacs: The
    Case of Cîteaux
Isaac of Stella: Sermons on the Christian Year,I - [II]
The Life of Beatrice of Nazareth
Serlo of Wilton & Serlo of Savigny: Works
Stephen of Lexington: Letters from Ireland
Stephen of Sawley: Treatises

—MONASTIC TEXTS—

EASTERN CHRISTIAN TRADITION

Besa: The Life of Shenoute
Cyril of Scythopolis: Lives of the Monks of Palestine
Dorotheos of Gaza: Discourses and Sayings
Evagrius Ponticus:Praktikos and Chapters on Prayer
Handmaids of the Lord: The Lives of Holy Women in
    Late Antiquity & the Early Middle Ages
    (Joan Petersen)
The Harlots of the Desert (Benedicta Ward)
John Moschos: The Spiritual Meadow
The Lives of the Desert Fathers
The Lives of Simeon Stylites (Robert Doran)
The Luminous Eye (Sebastian Brock)
Mena of Nikiou: Isaac of Alexandra & St Macrobius
Pachomian Koinonia I - III (Armand Vielleux)
Paphnutius: A Histories of the Monks of Upper Egypt
The Sayings of the Desert Fathers (B. Ward)
Spiritual Direction in the Early Christian East (Irénée
    Hausherr)
Spiritually Beneficial Tales of Paul, Bishop of
    Monembasia (John Wortley)
Symeon the New Theologian: The Theological and
    Practical Treatises & The Three Theological
    Discourses (P. McGuckin)
Theodoret of Cyrrhus: A History of the Monks of Syria
The Syriac Fathers on Prayer and the Spiritual Life
    (Sebastian Brock)

WESTERN CHRISTIAN TRADITION

Anselm of Canterbury: Letters I - III (W. Fröhlich)
Bede: Commentary on the Acts of the Apostles
Bede: Commentary on the Seven Catholic Epistles
Bede: Homilies on the Gospels I - II
The Celtic Monk (U. O Maidin)
Gregory the Great: Forty Gospel Homilies
The Meditations of Guigo I, Prior of the Charterhouse
    (A. Gordon Mursell)
Peter of Celle: Selected Works
The Letters of Armand-Jean de Rancé I - II
The Rule of the Master
The Rule of Saint Augustine
The Wound of Love: A Carthusian Miscellany

CHRISTIAN SPIRITUALITY

Abba: Guides to Wholeness & Holiness East & West
A Cloud of Witnesses: The Development of Christian
    Doctrine (D.N. Bell)
The Call of Wild Geese (M. Kelty)
Cistercian Way (André Louf)
The Contemplative Path
Drinking From the Hidden Fountain (T. Spidlík)
Eros and Allegory: Medieval Exegesis of the Song of
    Songs (Denys Turner)
Fathers Talking (Aelred Squire)
Friendship and Community (B. McGuire)
From Cloister to Classroom
The Silent Herald of Unity: The Life of Maria Gabrielle
    Sagheddu (M. Driscoll)
Life of St Mary Magdalene and of Her Sister
    St Martha (D. Mycoff)

CISTERCIAN PUBLICATIONS, INC.
TITLES LISTING

Many Mansions (D. N. Bell)
The Name of Jesus (Irénée Hausherr)
No Moment Too Small (Norvene Vest)
Penthos: The Doctrine of Compunction in the
    Christian East (Irénée Hausherr)
Rancé and the Trappist Legacy (A.J. Krailsheimer)
The Roots of the Modern Christian Tradition
Russian Mystics (S. Bolshakoff)
Sermons in A Monastery (M. Kelty)
The Spirituality of the Christian East (Tomas Spidlík)
The Spirituality of the Medieval West (André Vauchez)
Tuning In To Grace (André Louf)
Wholly Animals: A Book of Beastly Tales (D.N. Bell)

—MONASTIC STUDIES—

Community & Abbot in the Rule of St Benedict I - II
    (Adalbert De Vogüé)
The Finances of the Cistercian Order in the
    Fourteenth Century (Peter King)
Fountains Abbey & Its Benefactors (Joan Wardrop)
The Hermit Monks of Grandmont (Carole A.
    Hutchison)
In the Unity of the Holy Spirit (Sighard Kleiner)
The Joy of Learning & the Love of God: Essays in
    Honor of Jean Leclercq
Monastic Practices (Charles Cummings)
The Occupation of Celtic Sites in Ireland by the
    Canons Regular of St Augustine and the
    Cistercians (Geraldine Carville)
Reading Saint Benedict (Adalbert de Vogüé)
The Rule of St Benedict: A Doctrinal and Spiritual
    Commentary (Adalbert de Vogüé)
The Rule of St Benedict (Br. Pinocchio)
Serving God First (Sighard Kleiner)
St Hugh of Lincoln (D.H. Farmer)
Stones Laid Before the Lord (A. Dimier)
What Nuns Read (D. N. Bell)
With Greater Liberty: A Short History of Christian
    Monasticism and Religious Orders(K. Frank)

—CISTERCIAN STUDIES—

Aelred of Rievaulx: A Study (A. Squire)
Athirst for God: Spiritual Desire in Bernard of
    Clairvaux's Sermonson the the Song of Songs
    (M. Casey)
Beatrice of Nazareth in Her Context
    (Roger De Ganck)
Bernard of Clairvaux & the Cistercian Spirit
    (Jean Leclercq)
Bernard of Clairvaux: Man, Monk, Mystic
    (M. Casey) Tapes and readings
Bernard of Clairvaux: Studies Presented to Dom Jean
    Leclercq
Bernardus Magister (Nonacentenary)
Christ the Way: The Christology of Guerric of Igny
    (John Morson)
Cistercian Sign Language (R. Barakat)
The Cistercian Spirit
The Cistercians in Denmark (Brian McGuire)
The Cistercians in Scandinavia (James France)
A Difficult Saint (B. McGuire)

The Eleventh-century Background of Cîteaux
    (Bede K. Lackner)
A Gathering of Friends: Learning & Spirituality in John
    of Forde (Costello and Holdsworth)
Image and Likeness: The Augustinian Spirituality
    of William of St Thierry (D.N. Bell)
An Index of Authors & Works in Cistercian Libraries in
    Great Britain I (D.N. Bell)
The Mystical Theology of St Bernard (Etiénne Gilson)
Nicolas Cotheret's Annals of Cîteaux (Louis J. Lekai)
A Second Look at Saint Bernard (J.Leclercq)
The Spiritual Teachings of St Bernard of Clairvaux
    (J.R. Sommerfeldt)
Studiosorum Speculum [L. J. Lekai]
Towards Unification with God (Beatrice of Nazareth
    in Her Context, 2)
William, Abbot of St Thierry
Women and St Bernard of Clairvaux (Jean Leclercq)

—MEDIEVAL RELIGIOUS—
WOMEN
Lillian Thomas Shank and John A. Nichols, editors

Distant Echoes
Peace Weavers
Hidden Springs: Cistercian Monastic Women, 2 Vol.

—CARTHUSIAN TRADITION—

The Call of Silent Love
Guigo II: The Ladder of Monks & Twelve Meditations
    (Colledge & Walsh)
Meditations of Guigo II (A. G. Mursell)
The Way of Silent Love (A Carthusian Miscellany)
The Wound of Love (A Carthusian Miscellany)
They Speak by Silences (A Carthusian)

—STUDIES IN CISTERCIAN—
ART & ARCHITECTURE
Meredith Parsons Lillich, editor

Volumes II, III and IV are now available

—THOMAS MERTON—

The Climate of Monastic Prayer (T. Merton)
The Legacy of Thomas Merton (P. Hart)
The Message of Thomas Merton (P. Hart)
The Monastic Journey of Thomas Merton (P. Hart)
Thomas Merton Monk & Artist (V. Kramer)
Thomas Merton on St Bernard
Toward an Integrated Humanity (M. Basil
    Pennington ed.)

—CISTERCIAN LITURGICAL—
DOCUMENTS SERIES
Chrysogonus Waddell, ocso, editor

Hymn Collection of the Abbey of the Paracletee
Institutiones nostrae: The Paraclete Statutes
Molesme Summer-Season Breviary (4 volumes)
Old French Ordinary & Breviary of the Abbey of the
    Paraclete: Text & Commentary (2 volumes)

CISTERCIAN PUBLICATIONS, INC.
TITLES LISTING

The Cadouin Breviary (two volumes)
The Twelfth-century Cistercian Hymnal (2 volumes)
The Twelfth-century Cistercian Psalter
The Twelfth-century Usages of the Cistercian Lay
    brothers
Two Early *Libelli Missarum*

—STUDIA PATRISTICA XVIII—
Volumes 1, 2 and 3

❖ ❖ ❖ ❖ ❖ ❖ ❖ ❖ ❖ ❖ ❖ ❖ ❖ ❖

*Editorial queries & advance book information
should be directed to the Editorial Offices:*

Cistercian Publications
Dept. 96TLB
Institute of Cistercian Studies
Western Michigan University Station
Kalamazoo, Michigan 49008

Tel: (616) 387-8920 ❖ Fax: (616) 387-8921

❖ ❖ ❖ ❖ ❖ ❖ ❖ ❖ ❖ ❖ ❖ ❖ ❖ ❖

*A new 96-98 complete catalogue of
texts in translation and studies on
early, medieval, and modern monasticism is available now at no cost from
Cistercian Publications.*

Cistercian Publications is a non-profit cor-
poration. Its publishing program is restricted
to monastic texts in translation and books on
the monastic tradition.

*North American customers may order these books
through booksellers or directly from the warehouse,
(address below):*

Cistercian Publications (Distributor)
St Joseph's Abbey
Spencer, Massachusetts 01562

Tel: (508) 885-8730 ❖ Fax: (508) 885-8921